REDBACK 6

Other books in the Redbacks series:

Battlers and Billionaires:
The Story of Inequality in Australia
ANDREW LEIGH

Why We Argue about Climate Change
ERIC KNIGHT

Dog Days: Australia after the Boom
ROSS GARNAUT

Anzac's Long Shadow: The Cost of Our National Obsession
JAMES BROWN

Crime & Punishment: Offenders and Victims
in a Broken Justice System
RUSSELL MARKS

www.blackincbooks.com

SUPERMARKET MONSTERS

THE PRICE OF COLES AND WOOLWORTHS' DOMINANCE

Malcolm Knox

Published by Redback,
an imprint of Schwartz Publishing Pty Ltd
37–39 Langridge Street
Collingwood VIC 3066 Australia
email: enquiries@blackincbooks.com
www.blackincbooks.com

The National Library of Australia Cataloguing-in-Publication entry:

> Knox, Malcolm, 1966– author.
> Supermarket monsters: the price of Coles and Woolworths' dominance /
> Malcolm Knox.
> 9781863957304 (paperback)
> 9781925203257 (ebook)
> Coles Limited. Woolworths Ltd. Supermarkets—Australia. Grocery
> trade—Prices—Australia. Competition—Australia. Competition,
> Unfair—Australia.
> 381.4564130994

Cover design: Peter Long
Cover images: Alexey Buhantsov/depositphotos; JGade/Shutterstock

CONTENTS

INTRODUCTION

Woolworths and Coles are luminous successes of Australian enterprise. The two supermarket companies employ more Australians than any entity other than the state governments. Although this country provides just one fiftieth of the world's economic output and is home to one three-hundredth of its population, these two supermarket operators, whose business is mostly limited to Australia and New Zealand, are among the twenty biggest retailers on the globe, outsized only by the retail megaliths of the United States and Western Europe. Coles and Woolworths have, as Australians like to say of ourselves, punched well above their weight.

While Woolworths and Coles have not had to compete in global markets, unlike other Australian business successes such as BHP, Foster's, Westfield or CSL, their long march to the summit of a uniquely wealthy and isolated retail economy has been no meagre accomplishment. Once-ambitious rivals of Coles and Woolworths are now retail ghosts. The corporate self-esteem these two corporations take from their achievements over the past ninety years (Woolworths) and one hundred years (Coles) is merited. They have emerged, after a century of endeavour, as clear winners.

So theirs is not a story of rise and fall, but of rise and rise. Their histories may only be tallied in the currency of success. Some may like or dislike the supermarkets or what they represent, but that is hardly, in itself, the point facing Australians today. The modern corporation is programmed for creative destruction, and the strongest can no sooner be diverted from its destination than could the Terminator. The vectors that have brought these two companies to where they now stand are more akin to those of physics than of the humanities. As the University of British Columbia law professor Joel Bakan put it in his 2005 book *The Corporation: The pathological pursuit of profit and power*, 'The corporation's legally defined mandate is to pursue, relentlessly and without exception, its own self-interest, regardless of the often harmful consequences it might cause to others.'

It does not take a leftist critique to outline the simple amorality of the modern corporation. Milton Friedman said, approvingly, that a corporation's only responsibilities are to its shareholders and its customers, and its only driving force is to maximise profit. Whether it is valued positively or negatively, there is agreement on the nature of this machine. We are not asking if Coles and Woolworths have been true to their founders' intentions, or if they have failed in their missions. Those matters are settled. Instead, we pose questions about the consequences of their success: not whether these corporations are good or evil, but what the impact of their ascent on Australian life has been. What, in short, do these companies *mean*?

The most eye-opening feature of Coles and Woolworths is almost too obvious to comprehend: their stupendous scale. What are the consequences of having two supermarket chains that are so mind-warpingly enormous? There are many ways of apprehending this size, each with a capacity to stun the beholder. On average, every Australian man, woman and child, even taking into account those who never shop at Coles or Woolworths – the hospital patients, newborn babies, conscientious objectors and farmers living hundreds of kilometres from the nearest town – spends $100 a week on food, merchandise, liquor, hardware or petrol at an outlet owned by either of these two companies. Together, they take in more than 70 cents of every dollar spent in Australian supermarkets. That is how successful they have been, and it's only the tip of the iceberg.

They are even bigger than many of us realise. The $100 a week each of us spends at Coles or Woolworths is not limited to the supermarkets. It is the petrol and newspaper from a Coles-Shell outlet. It is the wine from Dan Murphy's and the beer from BWS. It is the fertiliser and hose from Bunnings or Masters. It is the clothes from Target, the toys from Big W and the towels from Kmart. It is the coins fed into the pokies at their pubs. Their meaning to Australian life lies not so much in what we spend in their outlets as in the diminishing possibility of spending it anywhere else.

As they have grown, they have converged. Statistically, they are almost mirror images: each has nearly 1000 supermarkets, nearly 700 petrol stations, more than 1000 bottle shops and hotels (making them the country's biggest poker machine operators), and more than 500 variety and hardware stores. All up, Coles (we will treat it synonymously with its parent company, Wesfarmers, of which retail operations form the major part) has 3383 retail outlets generating $62.3 billion in revenue and $2.7 billion in annual profit, while Woolworths has 3756 outlets generating $60.8 billion in revenue and $2.5 billion in annual profit. The share market values Wesfarmers at $51.2 billion, Woolworths at $43.5 billion. Together, the two corporations employ some 400,000 Australians.

Like anything too colossal and too ubiquitous to stand back from, Coles and Woolworths almost defy comprehension. Rather, we take them for granted. Trying to imagine modern Australia without them is vain; if there were not Woolworths and Coles dominating our malls and our suburbs, we could only conceive of the same giants with different names.

In recent years, there has been an unusual upsurge in disquiet over how the supermarket chains use their dominant positions. The bigger they have grown, the higher the anxiety. At some point, the public's perception of the growth of Woolworths and Coles tipped over from pride in local success to fear and suspicion of their size and power, and their names became lighting rods for populist campaigns against corporate bullying. In June 2014 Woolworths faced nationwide condemnation when farmers supplying fruit and vegetables for the chain were asked for a 'voluntary' contribution of 40 cents a crate, on top of a standard marketing payment of 2.5 per cent, to pay for a marketing campaign starring the British chef Jamie Oliver. Even conservative politicians were stirred, agriculture minister Barnaby Joyce saying the requested payment was 'a bit rich'. Oliver drew ridicule by saying he was only an 'employee' of Woolworths, even though his branding traded on the idea that he could sway a retailer's ethical decisions. Coincidentally but symbolically, the next week Woolworths had to recall thousands of defective Oliver-branded vegetable-shaped toys.

The Oliver-Woolworths story was part of a blizzard of adverse publicity for the supermarket giants. In the lead-up to the centennial Anzac Day of 2015, a public outcry forced Woolworths to withdraw an advertising campaign in which it associated itself with Anzac through the slogan 'Fresh in our memories'. Woolworths was hardly alone in exploiting the moment; in fact, it was hard to find an institution or major enterprise that was not. Yet such was the public's hair-trigger of unease over the supermarkets that Woolworths attracted much of the general hostility that had been building in the community over Anzac exploitation. This is the price Woolworths pays for its size: it is expected to behave in a manner fit for a national institution.

Meanwhile, Coles lost a series of court cases exposing the falsity of its claims to be selling 'fresh-baked' bread when the dough was in fact imported from Europe. Coles, whose previous chief executive Ian McLeod took home $19 million a year, entered into a dispute with $12-an-hour employees over a 5 per cent wage claim. Since the early 2000s, the Australian Consumer and Competition Commission (ACCC) had made a mission of its pursuit of Coles and Woolworths. It successfully prosecuted them over their ability to cross-subsidise their fuel discounts out of 'shopper dockets' from their non-fuel businesses – and when they were caught out continuing to do so, small business minister Bruce Billson floated the possibility of banning the practice through legislation, a rare rattle of the Canberra sabre. Woolworths was criticised by the Australian Medical Association and the Pharmacy Guild of Australia for using unqualified pharmacy students and nurses to offer 'health checks' to supermarket shoppers, and had been prosecuted for its part in a cartel case involving Colgate and Unilever over price-fixing. Woolworths was found, in reports by two banks, to have allowed substantial 'price creep' in the last quarter of 2013/14, possibly to pump up its earnings for the full year. Coles had been fined for misleading consumers over 'Made in Australia' labelling, while Woolworths' variety chain, Big W, had given $400,000 to children's charities after being found to have breached burn-free standards on pyjamas.

Throughout this drip-feed of bad-news stories, the big daddy of controversies was brewing: in May 2014 the ACCC commenced legal action against Coles for 'unconscionable conduct' in its dealings with suppliers, after a long-running investigation and evidence of sharp practice going to the very top – namely, McLeod's successor, John Durkan. In October 2014 the ACCC launched a second action, flowing out of the first, which suggested the bullying of suppliers was even more far-reaching.

As a charge, 'unconscionable conduct' was threatening for its very vagueness; because it was still seeking clear legal definition, it expanded to tarnish the company's reputation. A supermarket may not be liable its morality, but in the material that would emerge in the ACCC's case, acts of 'unconscionable conduct' went as close to corporate wickedness as many people would like to think. A measure of the reputational damage lay in Coles' decision to settle, paying some $10 million in fines and up to $16 million in reimbursements – a price it deemed worth paying to get the case out of the open courts.

While some of these controversies may be likened to spot fires that the supermarkets have done their best to put out, perhaps inevitable in businesses of such immensity, there is a thread that ties them together. Increasing numbers of Australians are uneasy about the size of the supermarkets, perceiving that Coles and Woolworths have grown so big that *whatever* they do to increase their profits, they cannot help but be marketplace bullies. The concern is that whichever way they move, they lay waste to fair trading.

In legal language, this distinction is represented in the debate between whether Australian competition law should be assessing anti-competitive behaviour by its *intent* or its *effects*. At present, the former test is applied: that is, companies can only be successfully prosecuted for anti-competitive behaviour if their intent has been to reduce competition. An alternative view, led by the former ACCC commissioner Allan Fels and recommended by the 2015 Harper Review into competition policy, is that the intent of companies' actions is not as relevant as their effects; that is, a company can have acted anti-competitively whether it meant to or not. This is a concern that comes up when companies have become so large that their profit-seeking actions will lead to a lessening of competition as a matter of inevitability; that they are bullies not because they want to be, but because their very size inhibits free enterprise. The question then arises – and it has been raised by a group of cross-bench senators gathering around the South Australian independent Nick Xenophon – as to whether courts should be given the power to order, as a penalty for anti-competitive behaviour, that too-big companies should be broken up.

These, then, are the parameters of the discussion in this book. Although one might react emotionally to stories of corporate bullying or overbearing tactics, the key questions are not located in the heart. A mountain of evidence can be amassed on both sides of the argument over whether Coles and Woolworths have acted as 'good' or 'bad' corporate citizens. The good-versus-evil debate, while appealing, is not only subjective but beside the point. It is not a matter of whether Woolworths or Coles intend to act as they do, but whether, given their size, they could act in any other way.

CHAPTER 1

KILLING THE COMPETITION

When Dominic White talks of the hardware stores that have died around Manly, on Sydney's northern beaches, he sounds like a zoologist listing extinct species. 'There was Hurstwaites at Balgowlah – that was going since the 1940s. Harders at Harbord, McIlwraiths in Manly, plus another two in Manly. There was Fairlight Hardware, Seaforth Hardware, North Balgowlah Hardware, two in Brookvale, Collaroy Hardware, Narrabeen Hardware, Wheeler Heights had one, and there was Hayman and Ellis in North Manly . . .' White fingers his grey moustache and pauses to think. 'That's all I can remember, but there may be one or two more.'

The beaches were, and still are, a tradies' hub. When the surf is up, clients receive calls postponing jobs and the beach car parks fill with vans and pick-up trucks. But when they are at work and buying supplies, the tradesmen and home handymen are more likely than ever to bump into each other. What was an ecosystem of fifteen hardware stores is now winnowed down to one Hardware & General and three giant green big-box Bunnings, which is owned, like Coles, by the West Australian conglomerate Wesfarmers. The Bunnings at nearby Brookvale, which obliterated most of the competition there, has in its turn been bombed by a new super-Bunnings which opened in December 2012, just one kilometre away in Manly Vale.

White's Mitre 10 franchise in North Manly was the last local independent to go, closing fifteen months after the super-Bunnings opened. 'General trading conditions had worsened since the first Bunnings,' he says, 'but when the second Bunnings came, that was it. Coles and Woolworths want to own everything. People might think they're supermarkets, but they're the petrol stations, the convenience stores, the bottle shops, the hardware stores, and everybody else is going out of business.'

For fourteen years from 2000, White's franchise was a crossover hardware hub for tradies and the public. The twenty-five full-time staff knew customers' names and were available to find products and help load them. When Bunnings moved into Warringah Mall, a two-minute drive to the north, it asked suppliers to sign exclusive agreements stopping them from selling to Mitre 10. The contracts were long-term and lucrative, initially at least, and hard to resist. 'The suppliers were sinking everything into Bunnings,' White says, 'which was what they wanted at first, but then Bunnings screwed them down so they couldn't make a buck, and they couldn't make it competitive by selling to anyone else either.'

Then the second Bunnings came, and from late 2012 White's store suffocated in a Bunnings sandwich. 'The second one has really hurt the first one, but they don't mind that if they put everyone else out of business,' he says. This path, known as brand-bombing, has been well-trodden in the United States, as Naomi Klein documented in her 2000 book *No Logo*. Big-box retailers, she wrote, 'spread like molasses: slow and thick'. They saturate areas to save on distribution costs and obviate the need for advertising. 'Category killers' such as Bunnings will cluster – think of how Starbucks saturated urban American locales – and cannibalise everything, including themselves; it's a Darwinian ecology that eventually leaves one giant, dictating terms. Winner take all.

It is effective business; Coles and Woolworths have been masters at eliminating competition since they were founded. There is an irony in the current debate over whether corporate behaviour has an intent or an effect of eliminating competition, because it is precisely in such elimination that Coles and Woolworths have excelled, within the bounds of the law, for the past century. Dominic White is a recent victim, but, with his long local memory, he knows he is far from the first.

Both Coles and Woolworths were established not as supermarkets but as general merchandise stores. In Coles' case, a multigenerational family legacy lay behind its first Melbourne stores. During the Victorian gold rushes,

George Coles grasped that there was better money to be made as a storekeeper to the trail of prospectors wending their way, in their thousands, from Port Phillip to the fields of Ballarat. Finding gold was a chancy business, but selling supplies to gold-seekers was true and sure. The Coles family prospered as general storekeepers until George's ambitious grandson George (G. J.) travelled to the northern hemisphere just before World War I to study big-city retail. He picked up on ideas such as 'one-stop shopping', money-back refunds and highly planned store layouts. When he returned to Melbourne in 1914, G. J. opened his first eponymous store in Smith Street, Collingwood, the foundation stone of the modern Coles company.

Inside a decade, G. J. Coles unveiled eight more stores in Melbourne. With £1 million in issued capital, Coles was floated on the stock exchange in the boom year of 1927. The infusion of funds enabled it to open its tenth store, in Sydney, a year later. The Great Depression did little to slow the chain's progress. Coles began selling its first own-brand merchandise, called Embassy, in 1929, and in 1930, when unemployment was heading to 25 per cent, the flagship Coles Book Arcade was unveiled in Bourke Street, Melbourne. It was Coles' twelfth store.

While Coles was firmly rooted in Victoria, the chain of stores that was to become its great rival started later and spread through the states more rapidly. Woolworths Stupendous Bargain Basement opened in Imperial Arcade, between Pitt Street and George Street in the centre of

Sydney, in 1924. The title was a direct steal from F. W. Woolworths, the American general merchandise chain which had more than a thousand outlets around the world but had not registered the trade name in Australia. The hopeful investors in the Australian Woolworths went to the public immediately, offering 25,000 shares to the market. They only attracted twenty-nine subscribers and a total of £11,707, but they were defiantly ambitious, expanding into Queensland in 1927, Western Australia in 1928, Victoria in 1933, South Australia in 1936 and Tasmania in 1940.

In the wake of the Depression, Woolworths and Coles were two of a galaxy of Australian general merchandise stores, most of which were single-outlet operations with strong local connections to country towns and the new suburbs of the capital cities. Retail was one sector of the economy that had grown through the 1930s, but by the middle of the decade there was already public unease about some of the chains' expansion and market power. In 1936 the New South Wales parliament appointed Justice Joseph Browne of the Industrial Relations Commission to inquire into the practices of chain stores. Coles was accused of using 'sweated' (or sweatshop) labour, underpaying employees and taking unfairly high profit margins from its sales, but the Browne inquiry cleared it. It would not be the last time Coles was examined for abuses of its market power.

The Second World War, which hurt chain stores more

than the Depression had, nevertheless proved a boon for the strongest survivors. Pre-war expansion had taken place rapidly, and many chains, having bought real estate and built new stores in the late 1930s, found themselves in distress in an era of shortages and rationing. Coles and Woolworths pounced, buying troubled competitors and converting defunct chains into their own stores. This acquisition drive accelerated at the war's end. Between 1949 and 1955, Coles bought rivals such as Neway Cash and Carry, Hoskins Stores, Selfridges, Gilray Stores, F&G, Mantons and Penneys. Annual sales rose from £7.5 million to £46 million in the decade from 1947 to 1957, by which stage Coles was employing more than 8000 workers. Woolworths was not far behind, with 200 outlets in its name by 1955, the year it opened its first Big W store.

Until then, neither chain sold food, preferring to consolidate their strengths in general merchandise. The reason was that neither chain saw itself as capable of sourcing, preserving and selling fresh food. It was only the advent of better packaging and preservatives that persuaded Coles and Woolworths to move into canned and packaged foods in the mid-1950s. In what was swiftly becoming a pattern, they made the move within months of each other. Woolworths introduced food at its store in Beverly Hills, Sydney, in 1955, and Coles followed with its first self-service store at Balwyn, Melbourne, in 1956.

Within three years of Woolworths' first foray, 7 per cent of Australian food was being sold in packaged form through supermarkets. Food was the future. In 1957 Woolworths made a coordinated leap into the groceries business by purchasing the Brisbane Cash & Carry chain. A year later Coles bought the 54-store Dickins chain. In 1960 Coles beat Woolies in the contest to buy the 253-store Matthews Thompson chain of food retailers, and re-branded the purchased stores as Coles Food Markets. Woolworths responded that year by opening its first 'com-prehensive supermarket' – the model for today's outlets, with cash registers and a wide range of discounted goods – at Warrawong in Wollongong. Two years later, the first Coles New World supermarket opened in Frankston, Mel-bourne, with 20,000 square feet of food and merchandise. The same year it moved into television promotion, spon-soring the *Coles £3000 Question* quiz show, a marketing precursor to today's *MasterChef*: advertising stores through association with popular television programs.

Although their expansion strategies and basic driving principle – achieve lower prices through bulk buying – were virtually identical, Coles and Woolworths had iden-tified each other as spiritual enemies. Perhaps, after thirty years of parallel growth in pursuit of the same markets, the similarity of purpose made a cultural collision inevi-table. For a decade from 1956, Coles and Woolies played an annual Australian rules football match. It was discon-tinued after excessive violence, the picnic days degenerat-ing into a bloodbath, with players punching and kneeing each other as payback for suspected dirty retail tricks.

The annual game was discontinued around 1966.

Destroying or buying the competition proceeded apace. In 1965 alone Coles opened fifty-four new supermarkets and crested 20,000 employees, generating £114 million in total sales. Within another two years, supermarkets overtook variety stores as the main drivers of Coles' income. But Coles was not leaving general merchandise behind. In 1968 it revived its variety wing by going into a joint venture with the American chain Kmart. By end of the 1960s Kmart had opened a total of 551 Australian stores.

Although the Coles and Woolworths executives were hostile to each other, differentiation did not follow. Mutual imitation embedded itself in both companies' cultures. 'Coles and Woolies' entered the lexicon, as if there was no difference. Today, a derisive term – 'Colesworths' – bunches them together. Monash University professor Stephen King, a former ACCC commissioner, says 'it's hard to see how they have differentiated themselves. Woolworths was behind Coles in the 1980s, but then branded itself the "Fresh Food People", took on the apple logo, and overtook Coles. What Coles then did was copy the strategy. More recently, Coles' "Down Down" campaign on lower prices was successful, and Woolies was soon doing exactly the same [its campaign is called "Cheap Cheap"; a parrot could not say it better]. If one does something that works, the other says, "We're not going to let you do anything different."' In January 2014 Woolworths made Oliver its marketing face. Within days Coles had unveiled Heston Blumenthal. One

British celebrity chef for another: that's differentiation.

Mimicry worked; through the decades, copycat tactics engorged the duopoly. Woolworths' and Coles' combined share of the Australia-wide supermarket trade hovered around 40 per cent in the 1970s and rose past 50 per cent in the mid-1980s. In 1985 Woolworths acquired the rival Safeway chain, which had operated since 1920 (predating its new parent). Two years later, in 1987, Coles bought the Bi-Lo supermarket chain.

The Coles family had been strict Presbyterians, and even though they had come into possession of liquor licences with the Matthews Thompson purchase, they didn't use them until 1971, when the Coles New World store at Warrnambool, in Victoria, became the first to sell alcohol. In 1981, converted to grog, Coles bought the 54-store Claude Fay Cellars chain, and soon afterwards the Liquorland chain, which then comprised just fourteen stores. When it added to its portfolio by buying the fourteen-store Target variety chain in 1982, Coles became the largest private employer in Australia. Its liquor business continued to grow, through the expansion of Liquorland and the setting up of the Vintage Cellars and First Choice chains, but Woolworths was quick to step in: its BWS and Dan Murphy's outlets would take the market lead away from Coles.

Only the paper-shuffling games of the 1980s could stop the two companies from following each other like racing yachts in a tacking duel. In 1985 Coles learnt that

Woolworths was planning a raid on the Myer department store chain, Australia's third-biggest retailer. Coles jumped in with a higher bid, taking over Myer, becoming the world's second biggest retailer outside the United States, with 127,000 employees and 1300 outlets generating $10 billion in sales. Coles Myer Ltd listed in London in 1987 and in New York in 1988.

Woolworths, for once, was travelling in the opposite direction. In 1989 Ron Brierley's Industrial Equity Limited ended Woolworths' sixty-five years as a public company, buying it for $850 million. Woolworths only remained in private hands for four years before, fattened up through the success of its first 'Fresh Food People' campaign, it was relisted for the public in 1993.

Whatever the ownership of the corporate entities and the combination with department stores, the core supermarket businesses stayed similar, although the lead between the pair regularly changed. Woolworths, which had fallen behind Coles in the 1970s, surged in the 1980s, with the introduction of fresh fruit and vegetables, scanning, EFTPOS and 24-hour stores. Coles followed the tactics, but at corporate level was suffering from scandal.

The company's management had developed a reputation for excess over many years. A 1970s managing director, Sir Thomas North, had bought a house in Toorak and added a two-car garage, burglar alarms, a rear extension and other improvements at company expense, because the renovations were deemed necessary for 'entertainment'. Coles buying managers would routinely receive pallets of 'extras' from suppliers for their personal use. Such bribery was said to be part of the culture, an acceptance of excess that was not so apparent, if it existed, at Woolworths. In 1979 Coles bought a 'managing director's residence' at Templestowe, in Melbourne, and six years later loaned the then incumbent, Brian Quinn, some millions of dollars to buy it. Between 1982 and 1988, Quinn, who had been influential in securing the acquisition of Myer, and officers in the Coles maintenance department defrauded the company of more than $4 million to carry out home improvements on the Templestowe residence, which Quinn maintained were for the company's benefit. Quinn would be removed from office in 1992 and five years later was jailed for fraud. He served two and a half years before his release.

While Coles Myer struggled, its supermarket division kept the public company afloat in the 1990s, even if it lagged behind Woolworths. At the end of the twentieth century the companies' combined percentage market share had steepled to the mid-70s (and up to 90 per cent in some regions). The deregulation of trading hours, bipartisan political enthusiasm for a National Competition Policy following the Hilmer Report, and the shrivelling of the third-biggest supermarket chain, Franklins, turned every week, for Coles and Woolworths, into Christmas week. Further opportunities arose in 1996, when an ACCC decision to permit the petrol chains Ampol and Caltex to merge created openings for new players. Woolworths was the first to dive in, entering the petrol/convenience store business in 1996, sometimes but not always in partnership with Caltex. Coles, joining forces with Shell, followed in 1997. Within a decade, Woolworths and Coles were taking a combined 48 per cent of Australian petrol sales – 24 per cent each.

By the mid-2000s, Woolworths and Coles formed a two-headed monster in the middle of the supermarket, liquor, petrol and general merchandise businesses. 'They both head towards the middle of the market,' King says. 'The intensity of their competition in the middle has made it very hard for anyone else to get in there.' While Coles and Woolworths continued to grow together, new entrants scrapped for the 'third force' space left by Franklins. The financially stressed Metcash currently franchises 1400 independent IGA outlets and the new German entrant Aldi has a fast-growing 350 outlets. America's Costco has five. Together, they have less than 20 per cent market share, although, as we shall see later, Aldi is becoming perhaps the first competitor to upset the Colesworths applecart.

Coles' most recent corporate reshuffle stabilised the company and began a new turn of the wheel that would reshape Australian life. In 2006 Coles spun off its Myer department stores to private equity for $1.6 billion. Coles, through its supermarkets, liquor and petrol stores, had 3000 outlets, but its annual sales had fallen from $22 billion to $17 billion since 2000. Its annual profit of $475 million was less than half that of Woolworths. In 2007 the West Australian conglomerate Wesfarmers offered $19.7 billion for Coles, setting up the largest corporate takeover in the country's history. To many analysts, it was a bold – meaning rash – bid from a company known for its conservatism in its specialities of agricultural engineering equipment and insurance. But Wesfarmers had a history in retail, too, and was doing very well with its Bunnings chain. It figured it had worked out a model that it could apply to supermarkets and set off in pursuit of the undisputed leader, Woolworths. When Wesfarmers' acquisition of Coles was bedded down in early 2008, the next transformation of contemporary Australian retail was set to gather pace.

To witness how hard it is to compete with Coles and Woolworths, it may be fruitful, rather than examining those, like Dominic White, who have fallen by the wayside, to look at those who have achieved some measure of success.

The Nikitaras brothers' corner store in West Hobart has a hallucinatory shine, like a stage set from a period movie. Staff in navy blue uniforms and white net caps smile from behind jars of preserved clementines, glacé peaches, pineapples and cherries. Glass cases present dioramas of stuffed olives, mushrooms and peppers; above them hang fragrant salamis; the shelves are packed with Tasmanian wine and crusty loaves. In the fresh vegetables section, greens glisten and truss tomatoes blush. Yet this is not some niche big-city organic haven; the shoppers filling their baskets with canned tuna, washing powder and packs of nappies are a reminder that this is an old-fashioned neighbourhood supermarket, a family grocer the way it used to be.

Marco, Nick and Nektarios Nikitaras grew up behind the counter of their Greek immigrant parents' shops. Marco married into another corner-store family, and the Nikitaras brothers took over a shop Marco's in-laws owned in Hill Street, West Hobart. Now the brothers are simultaneously the throwbacks and the cheeky upstarts of the Tasmanian grocery business. While a truly old-fashioned store, Hill Street Grocers also has its own petrol-voucher discounts and loyalty schemes. It is a mini-chain, with three outlets. It is an outpost of independence amid the highest density of Woolworths and Coles supermarkets in Australia.

Look closely, and something has gone amiss with the laws of scale: the checkouts are busier at Hill Street Grocers than at the desperate-feeling Woolworths a few hundred metres away. The fruit is both better-tasting *and* cheaper. There is no way this place should exist. Where did it all go so right?

In their upstairs office, Marco and Nick admit that their success is something of an illusion. 'We win battles,' Marco says, 'but we're losing the war.' They win through the quality of their produce and service, but they are losing behind the scenes, in the farms and the fields, where their supermarket rivals are cutting down their supply options and changing the way Australian food is produced. A decade ago the area in which the Nikitaras brothers sourced their fruit and vegetables, which surrounded Hobart but extended to most of Tasmania, had twelve lettuce growers; it now has two. Across all food production, those who supply supermarkets have enlarged and consolidated, while many others have gone, as have the food varieties they used to grow. 'There's no broccoli, field tomatoes, Roma tomatoes, there are only two substantial cherry growers, the raspberry growers have consolidated and gone to Woolworths,' Marco says. 'Lots of [varieties of] beans used to be grown, but not anymore. The supermarkets have exact specifications for the fruit and vegetables they want, and if they don't want them, the growers won't grow them.' This has centralised and narrowed the growing of food to a small number of supermarket-contracted juggernauts.

In Tasmania, for example, the Forth Valley-based Harvest Moon supplies Woolworths with tens of thousands of tonnes of carrots, all grown to fill massive time-sensitive orders. The only variety of beans supplied to the chains here are French beans. Australia-wide, most of Woolworths' French beans emanate from the 10,000 acres of the east-coast-based Mulgowie Farming Company, which also supplies the supermarket chain with 45 million cobs of sweet corn. Supermarket contracts have made these and other selected growers immensely successful and dominant, but have also checked the diversity of food production.

Distribution is also funnelled narrowly, nowhere more so than in Tasmania. Aided by a historical head start, having been established in Tasmania first, Woolworths enjoys tight relationships with its chosen food producers on the island. Meanwhile, Coles has found it more cost-effective to import its fruit and vegetables from the mainland. For shoppers at Coles in Hobart or Launceston, the idea of Tasmania as a food bowl is scarcely relevant as they purchase 'fresh' groceries that have arrived in the state in refrigerated containers.

In late 2014 Coles was caught out by the Advertising Standards Board, which ruled that the company had breached the food code with a television spot aired in August and September, in which celebrity chef Curtis Stone displayed Tasmanian pink lady apples and said, 'Feed your family better, fresher, with spring fruit and veg from Coles.' A Tasmanian viewer had complained to the board, writing: 'This is wrong and not possible, I live in Tassie and my apple tree is dormant. These apples would have been in storage for months, they are not fresh.'

Coles admitted that the apples were harvested in April, but cold storage technology permitted them to be promoted as 'fresh' four months later. 'Cold storage facilities place apples in a controlled low temperature and reduced oxygen (no nitrogen is added) environment to preserve their freshness . . . the apples are not frozen,' the supermarket said in a statement to the Advertising Standards Board. 'Coles considers apples can remain fresh, even if placed in cold storage. "Freshness" is determined with regard to the quality of the produce, not whether it has been stored or not.'

The board ruled that the problem was not the word 'fresh' so much as 'spring'. 'The board considered that the likely interpretation of the advertisement by the average consumer would be that the Tasmanian apples being promoted as fresh this spring would have been freshly picked in recent weeks and not over three months ago,' it said in its ruling. Coles was prevented from airing the advertisements again.

Woolworths' historical strength in Tasmania has meant, moreover, that it owns the island's only grocery distributor. A small competitor like Hill Street Grocer must pay Woolworths a commission for tinned goods, for example, brought in from Melbourne. 'Yeah, we are subsidising Woolworths!' Marco says with a grimace. Several times a month Marco flies from Tasmania to Melbourne, where he compares prices and seeks better deals. 'The situation here is contracting every day,' he says. 'You can't just go to a wholesaler in Tasmania. They choose you, or not, depending on their existing supply relations with Woolworths.' Most of the time it is too risky for a wholesaler to alienate Woolworths.

When you spend time at the Nikitaras brothers' store, it is obvious that food production, supply and retailing is more than an industry. The store is the beating heart of what Coles and Woolworths would like to be: a hub of fresh food people.

The supermarkets argue that the survival of a mini-chain such as Hill Street Grocers shows that the system is not a duopoly. But the Nikitaras brothers say they are the exception that proves the rule. For the daily quest for fresh produce, theirs is a DIY supply chain. Marco and Nick drive out to farms and truck in their produce themselves. They cut deals with 'micro-growers' – farmers who can operate at small volumes while, says Nick, 'they also have jobs as builders or millers or carpenters'.

And Woolworths is circling. To escape the supermarkets' stranglehold on Hobart – there are fifteen Woolworths and Coles on the western shore of the Derwent alone, servicing a population of around 100,000 – the Nikitarases started a store in tiny Lauderdale, a town of 2500 people to the south-west, seven years ago. 'There was no land zoned for big commercial uses,' Nick says. Lauderdale, on a narrow neck of land between the Derwent and Frederick Henry Bay, had been deemed too flood-prone for large buildings. 'We thought, that's a desert where we can create an oasis. We've built a popular community store. For five years, Woolworths has been after a site there. We've been through one expensive court process after another. They plan a 3500-square-metre supermarket 150 metres from us. If they open, we'll have to close. They will be unprofitable. They have no chance of profit for eight to ten years, but it's worth it to them to blow us up. At the moment we're quietly hopeful that they'll forget about it. But one day we'll arrive and there will be a huge excavator.'

The gravity-defying survival of Hill Street Grocers, which could only happen in a small city like Hobart, doesn't show that the Australian system is working, the brothers say; rather, it highlights the system's failures.

'What happens when you allow a duopoly?' Nick asks. 'Arnott's Biscuits is a good example. They have slashed their cost of production so low that their biscuits are all the same and taste of nothing. That's the effect. It's all to do with food production, whether primary or secondary. It gets reduced to the lowest common denominator. We have an American future: walk into the supermarket and see banks and banks of orange cheese.'

The brothers, like every player in a story about commerce, have a vested interest, yet their concern encompasses the very nature of food and food security in Australia. Steve, a lettuce grower with a big Woolworths contract (who therefore wishes to remain anonymous), says he is destroying more produce than he used to farm. Woolworths' orders vary in volume, but Steve has to be ready to fill the largest order possible. He has duly increased the size of his farm, but this means he is also destroying lettuces at a shocking rate. 'I have to grow for the maximum size of an order, or else I lose the contract,' he says. 'So I grow on that scale even though the order is usually a lot less. Everything I don't sell, I have to destroy.' Obviously, he can't sell it to small independent operators. While Steve's contract with Woolworths gives him security, his margins are tiny and are increasingly squeezed by rebates and marketing kick-ins. He was affronted by the request for 40 cents a crate for the Jamie Oliver campaign in 2014, but he went along. 'I didn't like it, but I can't afford to risk not paying,' Steve says.

Food destruction and the narrowing-down of produce types are, Nick Nikitaras says, among the hidden costs of cheap supermarket prices. 'Consumers make decisions based on price, and that's understandable,' he says. 'But I'd ask them to come to Tasmania and see where it ends up. Product lines and choice are reduced. There's more consolidation of growers, more importation, and eventually higher prices. It's insane from a food security perspective. Tasmania has incredible soil, unlimited water, a great temperate climate . . . and yet we're importing food.

'When people go into Woolworths and get milk for a dollar, they should also be asking, "What's the cost of this cheaper thing to the greater economy and its sustainability?" What are they really paying, behind that one dollar? That is a very expensive cheap product.'

It is worth unpacking the supermarkets' argument that Hill Street Grocers' survival demonstrates the healthy functioning of the market: there is room for everyone, they say, and consumers, by choosing an independent grocer, can keep the small players alive. The current managing director of Coles, John Durkan, has written: '[I]ncreased competition keeps us on our toes and keeps the whole industry jostling for the customer's spend – and that must be good for the customer. Plus, there are 30,000 independent grocers and food retailers in Australia, which means customers can always vote with their feet.'

Durkan was one of a cadre of British executives signed up by Wesfarmers when it took over Coles in 2007, and their mission was anything but the fostering of increased competition. Since BHP had shipped in Guillaume Delprat in 1898, a model of Australian business success has been to bring in expert managers from overseas. Advised by Archie Norman, the former British Conservative Party MP who had made his name turning around Britain's Asda supermarket chain in the 1990s, the Wesfarmers board hired Ian McLeod, a Scottish executive who had worked at Asda and was then managing the British retailer Halfords, to run Coles. On his first day in Perth, McLeod drove around Coles and Woolworths stores, and was dismayed by the difference. Coles stores were generally run-down and second-rate, whereas Woolworths were flourishing. Led by Paul Simons, Reg Clairs and later Roger Corbett, Woolworths had surged under its 'Fresh Food People' banner. Coles was often described as being in 'chronic catch-up mode'; its years under the former Brambles boss, John Fletcher, had been lacklustre. By the time McLeod arrived, Coles' turnover was $17 billion, compared with Woolworths' $37 billion.

McLeod assembled a clique of British retail managers to attack Coles' problems. Among them was Durkan, formerly of Safeway and Carphone Warehouse, who recounted, in Coles' official history, his initial impressions of the supermarket chain: 'The lack of investment was greater than I'd imagined, the availability of product wasn't good enough, cleanliness was an issue and things like broken slicers and malfunctioning ovens hampered team members trying to serve customers well. The first thing was to fix the basics; to renew and rejuvenate the stores and make Coles a place you'd want to go to shop. That took twelve to eighteen months to get under control.'

The story of Coles as a run-down chain lagging behind Woolworths in 2007, soon to be turned around under McLeod's management and to surge ahead of its rival, is now part of the Wesfarmers narrative. The importation of McLeod and his colleagues was a turning point in Australian retail history. What became known as the 'Tesco playbook' (it might as aptly be called the Asda, Sainsbury's or Marks & Spencer playbook, or for that matter the Walmart playbook) had arrived.

But it would be simplistic to attribute the current-day disquiet about the supermarket chains solely to the strategies adopted by Coles, and then Woolworths, from 2007. Before looking at the prosperity and also the trouble the McLeod era gave the industry, which we will do in Chapter Five, it is important to acknowledge that the public's wavering trust in the supermarkets pre-dated the Tesco playbook, and to look at the most visible areas of impact the supermarkets had on their communities: in their development of property and incursions into new territories; and in their treatment of their own people. As with any invading army, it was in these fundamentals – land and people – that the supermarket duopoly first made its presence felt.

CHAPTER 2

GRABBING THE LAND

Supermarkets may seem to spring to life spontaneously. Six months after a new Coles has opened, who can remember what was on the site before? But they are not divinely ordained. They open after months and years of careful planning and around-the-calendar work from strategists, researchers, property portfolio managers, business modellers and, copiously, lawyers. Every Coles and every Woolworths is where it is for a precise reason. Far from arising as part of some spontaneous natural order, many have had to overcome local opposition in order to exist.

If the march of the supermarkets were to meet a pocket of resistance, where else would it be but in the people's republics of north-eastern New South Wales, the hinterland communities home-grown from the spores of 1960s counterculture? And yet, even in one of Australia's most concentrated pockets of anti-corporate progressive local politics, the supermarkets have held sway, albeit by a roundabout route. In Mullumbimby, on the north coast of New South Wales, Woolworths prevailed not through aggressive expansion but by becoming the beneficiary of a Green–Brown impasse, capitalising when the opponents of big supermarkets became their own worst enemies.

With its timber/dairy/hemp heritage and cohabitation of old and new rural ways, picturesque 'Mullum' is a centre of slow food and small agriculture – and yet on its edge it has a Woolworths, as picturesque as a besser brick dropped into an ant farm. The story of how it got there is unedifying.

Since 1904, the Mallam family had owned and run the general store of the town, which is set in the northern rivers behind Byron Bay. Mullumbimby had evolved steadily until the 1970s, when its dairy farmers went into a spin over the arrival of city refugees, post-hippy dynasties, newagers, hobby farmers, retirees and surfers. Byron Shire, containing Mullumbimby and Byron Bay, now hosts a permanent population of 30,000 plus a transient and tourist community of another 5000 to 10,000. The majority live outside the two main towns. Mullumbimby itself is still home to just 3000 people.

In the 1990s, only Woolworths of the supermarket giants had gained a foothold in the shire. As the town of Byron Bay mushroomed, the Woolworths on Jonson Street became the unpickable knot of the town's daily traffic chokehold. While Byron had more than its share of organic and alternative food stores and farmers' markets, the

Woolworths was soon over-trading, unable to keep pace with a population convergence accelerated by the construction of a freeway linking Byron to Brisbane. For supermarket competition, the Woolworths only had a small independent within Byron and a Coles in the town of Brunswick Heads, some thirty minutes to the north.

In Mullumbimby, as the outlying population grew, so did pressure increase on the Mallams' store and their two bottle shops. Guy Mallam, a solicitor whose grandfather founded the store, says, 'The crucial issue [by the 1990s] was that we were trading in an old family property, a general store that had been converted into a supermarket. It was trading well enough, but the premises weren't big enough or efficient enough for a modern supermarket, and we needed to expand to trade properly.'

The family sought and found land on Station Street, on the eastern edge of Mullumbimby where the railway passes the town, and proposed building an expanded independent supermarket. They took their plans to Byron Shire Council. 'We had a sympathetic hearing and did our environmental reports,' Mallam says, 'but then there was a council election. The Greens got a majority and our proposal was knocked back.'

In defence of small retail, the spirit of the community, as represented by Greens councillors, set about a drawn-out process of obstructing the Mallams' planned expansion. The councillors didn't want *any* bigger supermarket. But in obstructing the devil they knew, the Greens were on a course towards letting in the devil they didn't.

After Byron Shire Council's rejection of Mallam's development application, the then New South Wales planning minister, the Labor Party's Frank Sartor, used his discretionary powers to consent to it; the state government's Far North Coast Regional Strategy had designated Mullumbimby a 'major growth' town. After that decision, Byron Shire Council raised procedural objections and asked Mallams for fees that ultimately amounted to $1.7 million, according to Guy Mallam.

Meanwhile, Woolworths sat back and watched from a distance. Overstretched in Byron Bay, the company saw opportunity in Mullumbimby. 'Woolworths came to us and said, "If you blokes ever get sick of the council, we would be interested in talking to you,"' Mallam recalls. 'They were watching everything. Their intelligence on what was going on was pretty good.'

The contest between the Mallam family and the council dragged on for six years. 'We constantly had to recalculate figures, and the family was getting older,' Guy says. 'We had to ask: did we really want it? We didn't have the resources to fight the council indefinitely. And Woolworths were always there in the background, asking if we were sick of the council yet. We were worried that if this kept going on, they would come in as opposition and destroy us. We eventually agreed to talk to them and agreed to sell to them.'

Woolworths bought Mallams out – the land, the development application, even the bottle shops in the town centre (which would become BWS outlets). It was at that late stage, realising Woolworths had outmanoeuvred everyone, that the community mobilised. Tricia Shantz, who was a member of the Mullumbimby Forum group, recalls organising 'not with the intention of opposing Woolworths, but giving the people of the town the opportunity to make an informed decision'. The group placed weekly bulletins in the local newspaper, the *Echo*, and conducted a telephone survey that found 50 per cent of Mullumbimbyites opposed the Woolworths, while 25 per cent supported it and 25 per cent were unsure. They wrote to the Woolworths chairman, the late James Strong, and its chief executive, Michael Luscombe, asking for a meeting.

They did not obtain it, but were contacted by Woolworths' government relations manager, Simon Berger (a prominent Liberal Party member who would be sacked by Woolworths in 2012 for his role as master of ceremonies at the Liberal function where Alan Jones said Julie Gillard's late father 'must have died of shame', and where a suit made from a chaff bag and signed by Jones was auctioned). According to Shantz, Berger was open to the idea of a public referendum in Mullumbimby, if the community could organise it. Berger hinted that Woolworths would abide by the result. 'We thought we had them on the run,' Shantz said, but the cost of organising and mounting the referendum to the required standard ran beyond the community group's resources.

Woolworths eventually outspent and outlasted the

community opposition and also outflanked the council, winning final approval from the state government in 2009 to build a 3000-square-metre shopping centre. Concerns about sewage, noise and traffic were addressed, against a background of rising local scepticism. In 2010 the new Woolworths opened. It was more than one-third larger than the store the Mallam family had proposed.

'We never wanted to sell to them,' Guy Mallam says. 'But the doctrinaire position of the Greens forced our hand. While I'm sympathetic to a lot of Green causes, their doctrinaire elements were what did the damage to moderate causes. They ended up getting the worst of all worlds.'

Woolworths' winning tactic in Mullumbimby was to mollify local antipathy by opening a dialogue with community groups, meanwhile circumventing council by appealing to a higher legal authority. This has been a process employed by both the big supermarket chains throughout Australia. In Maleny, Queensland, a town with many demographic similarities to Byron Bay and Mullumbimby, local opposition counted for little when Woolworths did an end-run, going to the courts to obtain planning permission in 2007. When the hippy strongholds failed, what hope did middle Australia have?

Supermarkets don't just appear. Coles and Woolworths add a net sixty outlets a year to their portfolios. While they may judge that they only open in response to well-researched local demand, that does not mean new supermarkets, bottle shops and petrol stations are always locally welcomed. In fact, they are very often opposed, by residents, local councils, churches and police. In such cases, the supermarkets have employed legal muscle and an evolving set of strategies to turn the argument their way. Democracy, in the form of local government and community action, is a mere speed hump.

A supermarket opening is a grand event. On 25 August 2014 Woolworths opened a new store in Coolangatta, the fast-growing Gold Coast hub. Local dignitaries were on site, at the new Strand shopping centre on Marine Parade, to celebrate the 3666-square-metre supermarket, with its eighteen checkouts and enlarged 'Macro' section of 'free range, free form and organic choices'. Sixty-five new jobs were announced. Surfing legend Wayne 'Rabbit' Bartholomew was given a knife to cut a Woolworths birthday cake. Representatives of Coolangatta State Primary School and Coolangatta Surf Life Saving Club were on hand to accept charitable donations from the company.

This opening passed without great controversy. Woolworths, Coles and Aldi compete with each other in the highly developed twin towns of Coolangatta-Tweed Heads, and the new Woolworths was a welcome refurbishment of a decades-old store. Elsewhere, things have not always travelled so smoothly, particularly in the liquor business.

In 2011 Woolworths encountered concerted local opposition when it applied to set up a BWS bottle shop in the

Blacktown council area of western Sydney. The site was on Quakers Hill Parkway, in a strip mall where there was already a McDonald's, a Subway, a service station, an estate agent and a solicitor. Quakers Hill High School was 555 metres away, and the surrounds between the mall and the school comprised suburban blocks and a park. With the proximity of fast-food outlets, the school and the park, the strip mall was already a magnet for teenagers. A nearby shopping centre already had an independent bottle shop.

When Woolworths lodged its development application, Blacktown Council received nearly 1200 objections, including a 697-signature petition. Police, schools and churches put their names to the opposition. They argued that there was no need for another bottle shop, that existing outlets would lose custom and that the location of the proposed BWS was too close to fast-food restaurants, the high school and the public park. Blacktown Council rejected Woolworths' application, and Woolworths appealed to the Land and Environment Court, where, the court recorded, the company 'disputes the Council's description of McDonald's as a significant youth attractor, and its description of the premises being proximate to the reserve and to the high school'. Woolworths offered to build a fence separating the BWS from the park, and argued that it was being discriminated against in favour of the existing bottle shop.

In her judgment, Linda Pearson, commissioner of the LEC, concluded: 'The evidence is that all liquor outlets can potentially supply alcohol to minors through secondary supply and that would not be a proper basis for refusal, and that the evidence does not support the Council's submission that the context of the site makes the level of risk unacceptable . . . There was no dispute that underage drinking and its potential social harms, and the general propositions about the extent, and risks . . . are of significant concern within the community, and are relevant in undertaking an assessment of whether the proposed development is likely to have an adverse social impact in the locality. While accepting that there are serious issues relating to underage consumption of alcohol and secondary supply of alcohol to minors, in my view the possibility that people might purchase alcohol from the proposed premises and supply that alcohol to underage children would not of itself be a basis for concluding that the proposed development is likely to have an unacceptable adverse social impact. There are sanctions associated with the sale, and secondary supply, of alcohol to minors.'

So Woolworths won. To paraphrase the Land and Environment Court, if kids are buying grog illegally from bottle shops, no extra harm will be done by setting up another bottle shop next to a McDonald's, a Subway and a school, because it's the responsibility of the bottle shop staff not to serve minors, and underage consumption of alcohol is society's problem, not Woolworths'.

Notwithstanding such apparently easy victories, the supermarket chains have not had it all their own way.

During the years that Woolworths was grinding down the Green opposition leading up to its store opening in Mullumbimby, it was concurrently losing fights for new liquor and petrol outlets elsewhere in Australia. Between 2006 and 2010 Woolworths went to court and lost in its attempts to open, among others, a Safeway petrol station in Wodonga on the New South Wales–Victoria border, liquor stores in Mornington Shire, in Victoria, and Harbour Town, in South Australia, and a Dan Murphy's liquor store at Currambine, in the northern suburbs of Perth. It is to that last case that we now turn, as it was in Perth that Woolworths developed and revealed new tactics.

Between 2007 and 2009 Woolworths was filing applications to the City of Joondalup, a fast-growing sprawl in Perth's north, to build a Dan Murphy's at Marmion Avenue, Currambine, on land part-owned by the Roman Catholic archbishop of Perth. Dan Murphy's was sweeping the nation with its successful formula of both cheap and expensive wines and a range of beers and spirits sold in warehouse-sized discount stores; it was giving Woolworths a strong lead over Coles in the liquor division. The Joondalup council refused consent, arguing that the liquor barn would destroy the amenity of the suburb, deface the shopping strip and encourage antisocial behaviour. Typically, the council's refusal was viewed by Woolworths as a mere setback in a longer game.

At the same time, Woolworths was trying to build another Dan Murphy's, 1800 square metres in size, in Perth's south, on the Canning Highway at Bicton, adjacent to the Melville Plaza Shopping Centre. The store would carry 4000 product lines, of which 3000 would be wine. Coles had one of its competitor liquor barns, a First Choice liquor store, in the same shopping centre, and Woolworths wanted to take them on in this affluent suburb, which it believed was a natural fit for a Dan Murphy's. But the West Australian Liquor Commission rejected Woolworths' application, questioning whether there needed to be another large alcohol store so close to the First Choice. The commission said it had to ask the public interest question: did the new store serve the public interest? It answered in the negative.

Woolworths appealed to the West Australian Supreme Court, which found that the Liquor Commission, by asking the public interest question, had effectively been applying a 'needs' test for consideration of a new liquor outlet. In 2006 the West Australian parliament had changed the Liquor and Gaming Act to take away the 'needs' test, which meant the liquor commission could no longer ask the public interest question. It was no longer permitted for the body that granted new liquor licenses to ask whether the surrounding community would benefit from one. The Supreme Court upheld Woolworths' appeal, even though, in support of its application, Woolworths had produced just eleven letters from the public and six from members of a wine club.

After all that, Woolworths did not end up building the

Dan Murphy's at Bicton. Instead, it landed five other stores south of the Swan, in Bull Creek, Cannington, Canning Vale, Southern River and Kelmscott, all within a ten-kilometre circle. Its win in the Supreme Court opened other doors. Back in Perth's north, Woolworths appealed against the Joondalup City Council refusal and won permission for its Currambine Dan Murphy's from the State Administrative Tribunal. It proceeded to build this one, while looking for a new site in the same council area. It found one in Joondalup central, 6.1 kilometres from the Currambine store.

On 19 December 2011 Woolworths applied to the West Australian Liquor Commission for permission to build this 1128-square-metre Dan Murphy's in Joondalup. When the commission rejected opposition from the public and moved in Woolworths' favour, the West Australian Commissioner of Police got involved, lodging a notice of intervention on 1 February 2012. The police commissioner was not objecting, but felt that concerns about antisocial behaviour should be taken into account before the Liquor Commission made its ruling.

In November 2012, when the Liquor Commission hearing recommenced, Woolworths showed how much more sophisticated its tactics had grown since the Bicton case. It provided reports from a town planner, an environmental consultant, a consumer researcher, a 'secret shopper' survey, a petition of 1675 people in favour of the Dan Murphy's, witness statements and a code of conduct, among other supporting paperwork. The Commissioner of Police submitted that the Dan Murphy's would harm 'the amenity of the locality' and that there were already sufficient liquor outlets in the area. Given the existing rates of alcohol-related harm, the police commissioner's evidence persuaded the Liquor Commission to refuse the application. In its reasons, the Liquor Commission noted 'the findings of a widely published and generally accepted body of academic research that has found a strong correlation between outlet density and alcohol related harm'. It accepted evidence that the number of bottle shops was associated with harmful alcohol consumption and that 'hospital contacts for anxiety, stress and depression' increased in proportion with the number of alcohol outlets. This was not a 'needs' test – the commission wasn't looking at whether Joondalup needed another big liquor store – but rather a more scathing rejection based on the undesirable impact of alcohol sales.

The rejection was a rare, and perhaps overdue, blow to Dan Murphy's expansion in Perth. Interestingly, Woolworths' arguments for the success of Dan Murphy's stores counted against them in the hearing. Evidence that Dan Murphy's had the best range, the greatest customer loyalty and a dominant market position, supported by six witnesses who said they would view a new Dan Murphy's as a 'destination' store in preference to other closer bottle shops, all looked good as a marketing pitch, but the Liquor Commission asked the obvious question: if there were already two Dan Murphy's stores within ten kilometres, at Currambine and Balga, and if they were so successful as 'destination' stores, why should there be another one? In November 2013 the Supreme Court dismissed Woolworths' appeal.

In South Australia the supermarket company's push to expand its liquor operations has outflanked local opposition by going to the courts. BWS stores complement Woolworths' Dan Murphy's operations: they are small, neighbourhood bottle shops that service foot traffic, whereas the typical Dan Murphy's barn comes with a massive car park to accommodate 'destination' grog shoppers. In 2012 and 2013 Woolworths won cases in the South Australian Licensing Court to open BWS stores at Smithfield and at Mawson Lakes, a one-time 'multi-function polis' on the northern outskirts of Adelaide. In both locations Woolworths faced opposition from community groups and existing independent liquor outlets, but was able to show the court that local 'needs' were not being met. In both locations the new BWS stores would be adjacent to Woolworths supermarkets. Here came the interesting part: when Woolworths managers told the court about the company's insights into changing shopper patterns.

In the Smithfield hearing, Paul Bonighton, the area manager for Woolworths supermarkets, said: '[T]he traditional weekly one shop has drifted away for most people and as we've all become busier and probably a little bit time-poor, our customers are wanting to come to us two to three and sometimes four times a week.' He then spoke of the relationship between a supermarket and its adjacent liquor outlet: 'Well, the way our liquor shops work, they're a part of our supermarket, so the customer that includes liquor in their purchasing habits when they visit the supermarket to buy a meal solution, whether it be two or three times a week, they're also purchasing what they need for that entertaining moment, whether it be a meal or friends over, so the frequency of visit for food purchase is lining up with frequency of visit for liquor purchase.'

In the Mawson Lakes hearing, Matthew Holland, Woolworths' senior regional property manager, said: 'People are becoming more and more time-poor and, as such, they are shopping more regularly in our stores, so they're not going – they're still doing a large, potential, weekly shop, with their $250 worth of family groceries, but what we're seeing more and more is smaller shops multiple times in a week, to grab fresh produce especially, everybody is so much more aware now of fresh produce, and there are so many more products on the market than there was ten years ago. So we're seeing customers coming to our stores more and more [times] a week.' Therefore, he continued, 'we believe that the provision of a bottle shop in the shopping centre will cater for people's needs significantly better than the Mawson Lakes Hotel. People will be able to do their shopping, pick up their groceries, bottle of wine and continue on with their business.'

These were significant admissions, albeit in the guise of corporate bragging. In much of Australia, supermarkets cannot sell alcohol, and at the time of the second hearing the South Australian government was considering changing the law to allow it. As the statements of Bonighton and Holland showed, Woolworths had already effectively circumvented the ban. The nearby BWS was 'a part of our supermarket', said Bonighton. The change in shopping patterns that had made Woolworths' push into fresh produce so successful were, as Holland said, sweeping seamlessly into beer and wine. The separation of supermarket and bottle shop (in Coles' case, the adjoining bottle shop is usually a Liquorland) was, in the supermarket's view, minimal – you come for your 'meal solution', the supermarket provides an 'alcohol solution' a few steps away – even though section 37 (2) of the South Australian Liquor Licensing Act stated that 'licensed premises must be devoted entirely to the business conducted under the licence and must be physically separate from premises used for other commercial purposes'. The physical separation, in many cases, was no more than a doorway.

Going by the testimony of Woolworths' managers, section 37 (2) had been successfully outwitted. Legally, the few steps from food to liquor meant the premises were 'physically separate', but from a marketing and practical point of view they were part of the same 'solution'. Independent supermarkets, bottle shops and winemakers saw past the fig leaf. When, in 2013, the South Australian government began feeling out the possibility of allowing supermarkets to sell booze, according to John Rau, the attorney-general and minister for business services and consumers, it was the independents who pushed for the change to the law as a means of evening the playing field: to them, Coles and Woolworths had already merged their food and liquor operations. 'Small to medium sized wine producers currently face difficulty in getting their wine on the shelves of retail liquor stores, which has a direct impact on their ability to access the retail liquor market,' Rau said. 'Following an approach from independent supermarket chains, the Government is exploring the proposal of a new liquor licence class . . . that would improve South Australian wine producers' access to the retail liquor market and assist the independent supermarkets in competing with larger liquor retailers (many of which are owned by the large supermarket chains).'

If you can't beat them, join them. As far as the independents were concerned, Woolworths and Coles were already selling alcohol through, or just next door to, their supermarkets, so the ban, having been beaten, had to be lifted.

Although the government was dressing up its proposal as being driven by small and independent producers and retailers, it was playing directly into Woolworths' and Coles' hands by legitimising what they were already doing. It was akin to a government dropping tax-avoidance laws because it had given up trying to control the biggest violators. Unsurprisingly, Woolworths was all for the change, stating in its submission to the government: 'For consumers, the sale of liquor in supermarkets would bring greater diversity, competition and choice to the packaged liquor sector. The proposal will also bring environmental benefit and greater convenience to consumers who currently require multiple shopping trips in order to purchase their food and wine requirements. Consumers will no longer need to undertake two shopping trips, with the associated inconvenience of finding two parking spaces, in doing their shopping. For time-poor shoppers and working families this is a convenient, common-sense and overdue regulatory reform that better reflects modern working lives and shopping habits.'

Heaven forfend that a supermarket shopper should have to make a second trip to buy their booze. And considering Woolworths' prior addition of thirty-three BWS stores to its South Australian supermarkets – which, perhaps inadvertently, it described as 'supermarkets with liquor' – the hypocrisy was disconcerting for anyone who hoped the law might have been taken seriously.

Woolworths even had the chutzpah to say that the change to the law would not help it so much as its independent competitors. In its submission, Woolworths pointed out that of its sixty-nine supermarkets in South Australia, thirty-six did *not* have a BWS. Of Coles' fifty-two South Australian supermarkets, twelve had adjoining

Liquorlands. And of the 238 independent supermarkets in the state, just seventeen, or 7 per cent, had bottle shops nearby. 'Therefore,' Woolworths concluded, 'while Woolworths supports the proposed reform and will be a beneficiary of it, most of the main beneficiaries of the reform will be the independent supermarkets.' A free-for-all on liquor in supermarkets would allow Woolworths' competitors the chance to catch up, it said. What it did not say was that the change would allow it to consolidate an already dominant position in the market.

Public opposition was vocal. Michael Thorn, the chief executive of the Foundation for Alcohol Research and Education, said, 'The country is awash with alcohol, nowhere more so than South Australia, and all the evidence shows us that increased availability will lead to even greater harms, increased rates of chronic disease, increased risky drinking by young people and increased domestic violence ... Allowing supermarkets to sell wine will increase availability of alcohol, resulting in increased harms.'

Minister Rau replied, 'We don't want to turn supermarkets into in effect bottle shops,' even though this was what the Woolworths executives had told the South Australian Licensing Court they were, 'in effect', already running. Food solutions and alcohol solutions, all solvent together.

Meanwhile, the same debate was running in Queensland, where Campbell Newman's government was proposing to drop its ban on alcohol sales in supermarkets. As in

South Australia, the independents were pushing for it. The Master Grocers' Association (the independent retailers' peak body) submitted that

> . . . a major part of the strength of Coles and Woolworths lies in their financial ability to control the market and squeeze their suppliers because the law allows them to do that. At the present time there appears nothing that can prevent the continued growth of Coles and Woolworths in the Queensland packaged liquor market with the regulatory structure that currently exists. MGA urges the Queensland Government to amend the legislation so as to open up a new opportunity for independent supermarkets to participate in the liquor industry. As an example – Coles (39 Liquorland) and Woolworths (96 BWS) have placed many of their detached bottle shops very close to their supermarkets – utilising their supermarket catalogues to advertise packaged liquor – this is an unfair competitive advantage!

Aldi also made a submission in favour of being able to sell liquor; it had previously done so in New South Wales, albeit in locked cases near the front of stores, and was free to sell alcohol in its Victorian stores. The Harper Review recommended further liberalisation of alcohol sales in supermarkets. For Woolworths and Coles, it was a story of the power of success: they had established a position of such market dominance that now their rivals and regulators were doing their work for them.

The alliance of Coles and Woolworths with their rivals to reform licensing laws would never be more than a marriage of convenience, but for all the enmity between the two major supermarkets, they have found common cause surprisingly often – when it has suited them. Indeed, one of the most enduring allegations of anti-competitive behaviour against the supermarkets is that they have worked together to clear the market of other players – to act, in short, as a duopoly. One of the most egregious cases of this was when they combined their liquor assets against independents.

The episode that started what would end up with the then largest court-ordered fine on the supermarkets took place in Campbelltown, Sydney, in 1998. The original Ettamogah Pub, an Australiana-themed bar in Brisbane, had branched out into Western Australia and New South Wales. Planning a new Ettamogah Pub and restaurant in Campbelltown's Macarthur Square shopping precinct, its owners entered into a ten-year lease with the centre's owners, Lend Lease. Ettamogah's manager, Leigh O'Brien, was aware that Woolworths and Coles had competing bottle shops in Macarthur Square (Mac's Liquor and Liquorland, respectively). Anticipating their opposition, O'Brien did not state in his original application that, after the establishment of goodwill, he might open a takeaway bottle shop, as had happened at the other Ettamogah Pubs. He obtained permission from Campbelltown's local council and police to open the pub, but ran into strong and, he thought, orchestrated opposition from Woolworths and Coles, which each raised numerous objections, almost total replicas of the other's. Each company then told O'Brien that it would withdraw its objections if he signed a deed of agreement conceding numerous restrictions – in effect, confining him to sell only Ettamogah-themed alcohol from a single point within the pub, and demanding he agree never to open a general bottle shop.

Correspondence grew heated as the opening of the pub was delayed. Anthony Smith, the Woolworths liquor manager running the opposition, wrote to a Woolworths senior property manager, Gary Reid, 'The danger for Woolworths *and Coles* [italics added] is that if this hotel/ pub falls over and is not the success [O'Brien] believes it will be then he could sell this licence to say a reputable hotel proprietor who could secure a site across the road from Macarthur Square and build a new hotel with a drive-in bottle shop/liquor barn. The removal of the hotel licence would be impossible to stop as it would be within the same neighbourhood. The bottom line is that we will protect our business wherever we can, and we are being more than reasonable in this case.'

O'Brien, in turn, complained in writing to Allan Fels, then the chairman of the ACCC: 'This is a classic case of the "big boys" trying to crucify small business. They are also suggesting/trying to make me sign an agreement and/or obtain permission first to sell my own products. Your support would be appreciated, please contact me if you could help in any way.'

The ACCC investigated, and found that not only did Woolworths and Coles have a case to answer for anti-competitive conduct in Campbelltown, but also that the same tactics were being deployed to thwart new entrants in other New South Wales locations. At Tweed Heads, on the Queensland border, Arncliffe, in Sydney's inner south, and Gosford, on the central coast, Woolworths and Coles were joining forces against new applicants in the same way. They objected to development applications, and then made it known, in concert, that they would withdraw their objections if the new applicant signed extremely restrictive agreements undertaking that they or future holders of their licences would never do anything that might compete with Woolworths and Coles – the two of them. Not only were the supermarkets demanding the new pubs never open separate bottle shops or drive-throughs, but they also insisted that the new licensees never advertise or promote over-the-counter sales, never home-deliver, never expand their premises regardless of customer demand, and only stock a limited amount of takeaway alcohol that both Woolworths and Coles agreed to. In their objections, Woolworths and Coles strenuously applied the 'needs' test that, ironically, they were later to dispute when arguing for a new Dan Murphy's or First Choice.

The ACCC's case was that Woolworths and Coles were engaging in what was, in effect, a shakedown, and that, having joined forces, their behaviour was anti-competitive. The law certainly allowed them to object to a new liquor outlet, but not to offer the new applicant a deal binding it to non-competitive behaviour, in exchange for withdrawing their objections, and not to combine their resources.

Indeed, given their history, the ostensibly surprising aspect of each of these episodes was how closely Woolworths and Coles were cooperating. The supermarkets denied that this was collusion, but the Federal Court's Justice James Allsop, in his final judgment, said, 'I do not agree. From the objective material as to Liquorland's conduct, the terms of the deed, the apparent commonality of approach and the straightforward approach of Mr Smith, I have no difficulty in concluding that Liquorland's [i.e. Coles'] purposes were in substance the same as those of Woolworths.'

Internal strategic documents surfaced to show the incentive Coles and Woolworths had for shutting out competition. Independent market research for Liquorland estimated that location was the most important determinant of where people shopped for alcohol in 77 to 86 per cent of cases. Once location could be secured exclusively, prices could be jacked up, as people would continue shopping at the nearest store almost regardless of price. A memo written by Adrian Harrigan, Liquorland's New South Wales sales manager, said that once exclusivity within a five-kilometre radius was ensured, prices on leading lines could be raised by 50 cents per item without any effect on custom, yielding a net profit increase of $2 million per store. Justice Allsop found that 'the lack of local direct close competition would allow Liquorland to "charge more or give less"'.

Finding that Woolworths had acted anti-competitively, Justice Allsop fined it $7 million. In a separate Federal Court action brought by the ACCC, Justice Roger Gyles fined Coles, through Liquorland, $4.75 million.

These remain among Australia's highest penalties for anti-competitive behaviour. Yet, as can be seen from the subsequent cases that decade, they did little to stop Coles' and Woolworths' advance in the liquor industry, and nothing to stop their overwhelming power in suburban shopping centres around the country. In fact, the lessons the supermarkets learned from their failure to block new competitors from setting up were used in their own later expansions. By learning, through their court defeats in the early 2000s, how new liquor outlets could start up, they gathered the tactics they would need to get their next applications through the courts.

Coles and Woolworths supermarkets usually don't need to go to court to get what they want in shopping centres. Through their market power, they occupy a uniquely privileged position. Market forces do the job for them.

Coles and Woolworths are not themselves shopping centre property developers – though Woolworths does have a small, loss-making development arm. But in the real estate they control, their suasion is greater than that of a mere landlord. As 'anchor tenants', the supermarkets rule the roost in most of Australia's 1350 shopping centres and malls. Landlords would be lost without them. If you wonder why small retailers struggle to stay afloat and there is a movable feast of little shops coming and going in your local mall, you need only look at the influence held by the anchor tenants.

While there are some big players like Westfield and Stockland, the ownership of shopping centres in Australia is spread among more than 500 separate owners, most of whom own just the one centre. However large or small they are, they face a common challenge, which is that they are extremely reliant on a secured anchor tenant. Indeed, finance for the construction of a shopping centre in the first place will be difficult to find without a secured anchor tenant. Whether the owner is Westfield or a country-town one-centre developer, the requirement for an anchor tenant is constant. If it isn't a supermarket, it must be a discount department store (such as Big W, Target or Kmart, owned by the supermarket companies), or, in rare cases, a department store such as Myer or David Jones.

Anchor tenants occupy up to 75 per cent of the lettable area in shopping centre developments, and draw in 80 per cent of foot traffic, but due to their bargaining position they can negotiate their leases down so that they pay, on average, only 20 to 25 per cent of centres' rental income.

As well, they benefit from inducements such as rent holidays, assistance with fit-outs, preferential facilities and other sweetheart deals.

The theory, from the owners' point of view, is that anchor tenants are big enough to attract customers for other shops, and their size will generate the majority of the centre's rental revenue; the other 75 to 80 per cent will be paid by the shops that dice up the remaining 25 per cent of the lettable area. The dependency of landlord upon anchor tenant is total. Anchor tenants will also take up leases typically of twenty to twenty-five years' duration, far longer than those of 'satellite tenants'.

The prospect of losing a long-term anchor tenant is enough to undermine any development, and because of this power, the anchor tenant can dictate terms. Sometimes this has resulted in them excluding certain other tenants from the property, which is illegal under the Competition and Consumer Act. In its 2008 Grocery Inquiry, the ACCC found that as many as 700 supermarket leases around Australia, in big cities and small towns alike, contained illegal restrictions on landlords, preventing them from leasing space to anchor tenants' competitors. 'A number of supermarket operators provided the inquiry with specific and credible evidence of leases between the major supermarket chains and shopping centres which, they contended, have prevented or delayed their entry into a centre,' the inquiry reported. 'The ACCC also used its information-gathering powers to obtain leases from Coles, Woolworths and shopping centre owners which confirmed that such restrictive provisions are often included in leases.'

Coles and Woolworths were not generally using these leases to shut out each other, but rather to damage independent operators. Coles, for instance, could insist on a shopping centre not also leasing space to an IGA, or it would withdraw as anchor tenant. Not only this, but Coles and Woolworths might also include such restrictions against competing liquor, hardware, general merchandise or petrol outlets. It was a club of two, the inquiry found: 'Coles and/or Woolworths are essentially considered almost "must have" tenants for any successful, large-scale shopping centre. Almost inevitably, where there are two large supermarket sites available within a centre and Coles and Woolworths both wish to be present in the centre, they will be offered the sites. While the preference of centre owners to have Coles and/or Woolworths as tenants is a reflection of their importance to the success or otherwise of centres, it does create a significant barrier to entry for other supermarket operators.'

The ACCC moved to end this practice in 2009, but with Coles and Woolworths still accounting for more than 50 per cent of some shopping centre owners' total income across numerous malls, concerns over the market power of anchor tenants led to a Senate inquiry, titled 'Need for a National Approach to Retail Leasing Agreements', which has heard that there is a 'war' between small tenants on the one side and owners, aligned with anchor tenants, on the other. If Coles and Woolworths are not working to shut each other out of shopping centre developments, their position as favoured tenants has led to inequities in terms that drive small tenants out of business. The flow-on effect of having a small shop near a Coles or Woolworths is more than offset by the ruinous terms demanded by the landlord – because the landlord is offering such generous terms to the supermarkets. The tendency towards big-chain retail in Australia is therefore accelerated by the power of Coles and Woolworths. If the big players can't be defeated or joined, they can be replicated. More and more, the 'smaller' tenants in Australian shopping centres are not independents, but chains. A future where Australian shopping centres look like British High Streets, dominated by a numbing repetition of Top Shops, Tescos, Boots, Sainsburys, Carphone Warehouses and the same rota of chain retail outlets in the same bland shufflings throughout the kingdom, is easy to imagine.

Mullumbimby's point of pride, before Woolworths, was that aside from two bank branches it had no chain retail. None at all. 'It's a small business town,' says Shantz. 'We were never opposed to big supermarkets as such, but we were asking the community if they thought a chain was appropriate in a town that they had built free from corporates.'

The community lost the battle there, but learnt several lessons. A year after winning the right to build on the fringe of Mullumbimby, Woolworths turned its eye back to Byron Bay and applied to transfer a liquor licence from Sydney to set up a Byron Bay Dan Murphy's. It now had some small-scale supermarket opposition, with an Aldi and an IGA in Byron. Liquor, there as everywhere, was where the growth was. But this time the northern rivers community opposition was ready.

In September 2012 a five-hour meeting of the Independent Liquor and Gaming Authority was held in public in Byron Bay. Police and the local hospital added their voices to concerns about an upsurge of alcohol-related harm in the shire, which already had more than 110 licensed premises. The authority refused Woolworths' application, and the Dan Murphy's never came into being.

'We were all really impressed with that result,' says Shantz. 'But the best favour that was done was that the local council had approved it. If they'd rejected it, Woolworths could have appealed and it would have been decided in the courts. As we know, even if public opinion is strongly one way, that's no help when these corporations take it into the court system.'

CHAPTER 3

SERVING THE PEOPLE

While running for the US presidency in 2011, Mitt Romney defended big companies: 'Corporations are people, my friend . . . of course they are. Everything corporations earn ultimately goes to the people. Where do you think it goes? Whose pockets? Whose pockets? People's pockets. Human beings, my friend.'

Woolworths and Coles would say the same. Trying to counter the wave of negative publicity that hit both supermarket chains in mid-2014, Woolworths introduced an advertising campaign that played to the warm emotions around teenagers getting their first job. It was a potent image: hundreds of thousands of Australian families have been there. My wife's first job was at Woolies in Kiama, on the south coast of New South Wales. As with many teenagers, then and now, it was a pocket-money job. Most supermarket jobs are transient experiences: more people *leave* employment with Coles and Woolworths each year than any other Australian private or government entity.

Even if corporations do not themselves have human characteristics, they are composed of people. There is an episode of *The Office* in which David Brent (Ricky Gervais) and his staff sit down to watch a 1960s-era motivational film. The host opens with the question, 'What's the most important thing to any company?' Brent, in politically correct mode, grins smugly at his co-workers and says, 'People.' They turn back to the old-school tape, where the host is holding up a fistful of cash and answering his own question: 'Profits!'

It's a neat piece of historical observation. Putting a face on business has been a signature shift of corporate culture in our time. Indeed, the term 'corporate culture' is another sign of that shift. Whether we belong to staff, customers, suppliers, shareholders, all subsets of that vogue group, 'stakeholders', we are supposed to feel more warmly disposed to a corporation if we are reminded that it is not just a mechanism.

The sixty-five jobs announced at the new Woolworths in Coolangatta in August 2014 were a drop in the ocean of how many people owe their living to supermarkets. According to the company, eighty-seven Australians enter employment with Woolies every day of the year. Only the state governments give work to more than the supermarkets' combined 400,000 staff. In the last decade annual reports have bubbled with photos and words about 'Our People', and both Coles and Woolworths emphasise the value they place on their workers. Given their enormous churn, Coles and Woolworths like to pay tribute to their long-serving employees, with prizes and stories in company newsletters. Wesfarmers provides 'a rewarding and satisfying environment for our 200,000-plus employees', chairman Bob Every wrote in the 2013 annual report, and has 'a moral obligation to ensure our employees go home safely at the end of their working day'. Managing director Richard Goyder wrote that 'very good people' are 'our only true competitive advantage'. Woolworths makes the same claim. Its board has a 'People Policy Committee' that oversees programs to increase employment diversity and opportunities for workers with disabilities, though the numbers are not overly flattering. Of Woolworths' 197,000 employees, just 1.5 per cent have a declared disability, and 1.25 per cent are Indigenous. Women make up more than half of the Woolies workforce, or 53.3 per cent, but only 30.3 per cent of executive positions. Coles' workforce is even more female-heavy, with 57 per cent, but only 28 per cent of those are in management. Four years ago, Coles employed just sixty-five full-time Indigenous staff in the whole of Australia, although this rose to 1000 after a recruitment drive.

When you want to know how companies wish to treat their people, the annual report shows what colours are flying from the flagpole. But retail work is often low-skilled, low-paid and short-term, not to mention nasty, brutish and short, and it is at this Hobbesian quotidian level that the practices of the supermarkets often diverge from their high-minded corporate mission. Chairmen and managing directors stand on the bridge of the ship, but it is below decks that the action happens. The top company officials don't deal with recalcitrant teenage shelf-stackers, drug-addled customers, shoplifters, overzealous store security guards, unhappy checkout staff or feuding forklift drivers. These are matters for the middle and lower managers, who are, in the practical sense, Woolworths' and Coles' real representatives. To see how they can behave, you need to visit their disputes.

At the bulk level of industrial relations, Woolworths and Coles negotiate wage agreements on a regular basis with the Shop Distributive and Allied Employees Association, the union representing low-paid supermarket workers.

In 2010 Woolworths and the Queensland branch of the SDA fought all the way to the full court of the Federal Court over long-service leave entitlements for employees who work non-recurrent afternoon and night shifts and Sundays. Woolworths wanted to gear their long-service leave to the basic 38-hour week, while the SDA argued that the workers should receive leave based on their actual wage, which was often higher than the basic award due to night and weekend loadings. This loading amounted to an extra $2.84 to $4.02 per hour. Woolworths lost the case at three levels of lower courts. Despite the niggardly dollar amounts per employee it was being asked to pay, Woolworths judged the overall materiality important enough to pursue the matter for two years up to the second-highest court in the land, where it lost again.

Over the following two years, Woolworths and Coles found themselves repeatedly in court with the SDA over the treatment of public holidays which had fallen on Saturdays or Sundays, quarrelling over whether employees were entitled to these public holidays or not. Woolworths and Coles were also in court with the SDA and the Transport Workers' Union over numerous unfair dismissal disputes. What can be concluded from the detail of these cases, whether they were ultimately won or lost, is that the supermarkets strenuously pursued and defended their legal rights against all comers.

The same is generally true of both companies' disputes with individual workers and customers. The supermarkets' legal advisers tend not to take a backward step. The work practices shown in the following examples are not the type of clashes that happen every day. But with companies, as with people, certain truths are revealed by how they react when things have gone wrong.

In 2009 Mario Sisko, a store manager at Woolworths Shellharbour, near Wollongong, was summoned to a meeting with a supervisor who had criticised his performance. Sisko, thirty-seven, had worked for Woolies for sixteen years. According to the company, just one in six

Woolworths employees has been with the company for more than ten years, although its website boasts of the career opportunities it offers those who stay beyond the casual shelf-stacking stage of life. Mario Sisko, in his sixteen years, had progressed from menial work to store management. He was the type of loyal, steadily rising employee about whom Woolworths boasts. At the 2009 meeting with his supervisor, Sisko heard a litany of complaints about his efforts. Then he went home and attempted to commit suicide.

Three years later, having been unfit for work since the incident, Sisko claimed in the Workers' Compensation Commission that Woolworths had caused him psychological injury through lack of support, harassment and bullying. The commission ordered Woolworths to pay Sisko his store manager's rate of $1269 a week for six months, and then approximately half that for the next three years, a total of around $150,000. Woolworths appealed, claiming Sisko's problems resulted from an addiction to narcotics, but lost.

Both Sisko's evidence and Woolworths' tactics were eye-opening. For a decade Sisko had worked at Woolworths Riverwood, in western Sydney, more than two hours from his home near Wollongong, and eventually he had been promoted to the role of store trading manager. A car accident in 1999 left him with chronic neck pain and depression. His wife was also taking painkillers after back surgery. But Sisko kept turning up at work and performing well. A Woolworths 'Individual Performance and Development Plan' in June 2008 said Sisko was doing a good job despite his health problems and his long daily commute, but that he needed to work on 'his eye for detail in fresh foods' after being picked up for leaving produce on display past its use-by date. A month later, having again been 'counselled' for not removing aged produce, Sisko asked for a transfer to the Wollongong area: he needed to be closer to home to look after his child and wife. In taking a lower-rated job at Shellharbour, he accepted a cut in position and salary.

After surgery for haemorrhoids in 2009, Sisko ignored his doctor's advice to take a month off work because, he said, he felt under pressure to go back to the store. The Shellharbour outlet was run-down, and Sisko covered three managerial jobs while his two immediate superiors were on leave. A visiting supervisor, Kathryn King, told Sisko that an upcoming internal quality audit was likely to assess the Shellharbour store as an unsatisfactory two out of five. Preparing for the audit and desperate to improve the store, Sisko worked long hours of unpaid overtime, grew anxious, ate one meal a day, slept two or three hours a night, suffered vomiting and diarrhoea, and argued with fellow employees in the rush to lift standards. For support, Woolworths sent him one extra unskilled trainee.

When the store manager, Manfred Kubitzky, returned from sick leave, according to Sisko's evidence, he pressured Sisko to manipulate records so the store would receive a five out of five in the audit. Sisko said that he refused, and Kubitzky reprimanded him. An upset Sisko reported this to his area manager but no action was taken. Meanwhile, the store trading manager, Juliana Sirijovska, who had also returned from leave, verbally abused Sisko for removing boxes from an aisle and then asked him to find a screwdriver from the service desk to break into the cash office, as she could not find the keys. When Sisko instead asked for a screwdriver from the bakery, Sirijovska yelled, in front of other staff, 'I told you to go to the service desk, not the bakery department. Don't you listen to anything I say?' Sisko replied, 'Shut the fuck up.'

This confrontation brought on a meeting in front of Kubitzky, who called Sisko a liar and asked him to apologise to Sirijovska. Sisko did so, but said he was 'not used to being yelled at from down the hallway like some imbecile'. Over the next month, more senior Woolworths managers came to Shellharbour to 'counsel' Sisko. One, Ron Carradine, told him, 'I don't give a fuck about the circumstances that have happened. You are an experienced manager and this should be a walk in the park to you.' Sisko said he would bring his department up to scratch within three months. Carradine said, 'You have fucking four weeks.'

Sisko went from that meeting to the toilet, where he vomited and cried. After several more incidents, including being criticised for taking cigarette breaks and being told he was a liar by another superior, Sisko went home on 21 May 2009 and swallowed a bottle of Valium pills.

He survived but was placed under sedation at Shellharbour hospital. His career at Woolworths was finished.

Woolworths went in pursuit of Sisko once he claimed workers' compensation. The Workers' Compensation Commission found that Woolworths misrepresented medical evidence in its attempt to show that Sisko's problems were caused by an addiction to opiates. The commission found instead that Sisko's psychological injury had been caused by bullying and overwork at Woolworths Shellharbour. Woolworths appealed. In his ruling, the president of the commission, Bill Roche, said Woolworths' case was 'without merit' and its legal tactics were 'most unsatisfactory'. In Shellharbour, the commission found, Sisko's managers had victimised him and hounded him out of his job, and now that he was claiming compensation, the Woolworths legal team was repeating the dose.

The Sisko case was far from the first example of Woolworths or Coles using the legal system to pursue their employees under the guise of protecting their legal rights. The supermarkets have spent millions in the courts fighting even their longest-term workers, some of whom had no history of difficulties with their employers.

Barry Buckland was a Woolworths undercover store detective at Orange, New South Wales, from 1997. On 2 December 2008, Buckland tried to stop six teenage customers from throwing balls around the aisles of the store. They pushed him to the floor and ran over him with a trolley. He chased them outside, where they assaulted him again. He sustained a shoulder injury but went back to work. A year later, Woolworths sacked him for 'serious misconduct' when he apprehended a female customer whom he suspected of shoplifting.

Buckland thought he had seen the woman stuff some underwear down the front of her trousers. Unable to physically apprehend her due to his shoulder injury, he followed her out of the store and asked another employee to stop her. The customer was taken to a room, where she was found not to have any stolen goods. The woman made a complaint and Buckland was summarily dismissed.

'My boss claims that I was wrong in apprehending this lady and went about it the wrong way,' Buckland told the NSW Workers Compensation Commission. 'I wasn't wrong and didn't do it the wrong way. I just followed normal procedure. The boss didn't accept that and I got the sack.' He felt that the management had been seeking a pretext to dismiss him, as his effectiveness had been limited since he injured his shoulder, even though that injury was incurred while he was performing his duties on the supermarket's behalf. Buckland won his compensation claim, the commission finding Woolworths had not followed its duty of care. Later, it dismissed Woolworths' appeal.

In the Victorian County Court in 2011, Woolworths tried to show that an employee named Ian Douglas Warfe was faking an elbow injury. Warfe had worked for the company for seventeen years, and was a manager at a Safeway in the town of Lara when diagnosed with tennis elbow in both arms. Prior to Lara, Warfe had worked for Woolworths at another country town, Drysdale, where, according to court documents, a manager named Cohen 'constantly abused him, threw items at him, including glass bottles, and put him down'. When Warfe left employment at the store, Cohen allegedly said, 'I finally got rid of the bastard.' Depression and anxiety followed, and Warfe moved from Drysdale to Lara, but, from 2004, he was unable to work due to his arm injuries.

In response to Warfe's claim, Woolworths attacked his character. It implied he had a history of faking injuries and hired private investigators to film him in outdoor activities. Woolworths' investigators shot seventy-nine hours of film of Warfe, of which it produced two hours for the court. County Court judge Kathryn Kings concluded that the unshown seventy-seven hours of footage must not have helped Woolworths' case.

A psychiatrist, Dr Francis Payne, told the court that Warfe's depression was consistent with the trauma he had suffered at Woolworths. Associate professor of psychiatry Maurice Wallin gave evidence that Warfe's incapacity to work could be lifelong. Woolworths produced doctors to testify that Warfe had no physical impairment that should stop him performing light duties in another job. Judge Kings disagreed, finding that Warfe had a case for compensation. Given his low wage, Woolworths spent far more contesting the case than they ultimately had to pay out.

In the same year, Woolworths also contested the

compensation claim of Marjolein Pushie, a fifty-year-old shelf-stacker who had tripped and injured her back while working. She was earning approximately $350 a week at the time. Woolworths lost there too. Again, the payout to Pushie was less than the cost of pursuing her. In exercising its legal rights, Woolworths has seldom followed a policy of keeping prices 'cheap cheap'.

On occasion, the legal pursuit continues even after employees' deaths. In 2009 Marie Scanlan, the manager of a Woolworths petrol station at Plumpton, in western Sydney, died of a heart attack. She had been working an average of sixty to seventy hours a week, sometimes for fourteen days straight, while being paid for a five-day, forty-five-hour week. Her family said she had asked Woolworths to supply staff to assist her, and enable her to take leave, of which she had three years' worth accrued at the time of her death. Woolworths contended that she had died because she was obese and unhealthy. The NSW Workers Compensation Commission awarded her three children $144,000 each. Woolworths appealed, and lost.

Those cases involved Woolworths, but, as ever, Coles has followed the same template. A Coles warehouse stock controller of six years' standing, Gary Homes, was dismissed from the company's distribution centre at Edinburgh, outside Adelaide, on 10 September 2013 for 'serious and wilful misconduct'. He had allegedly stolen one tin of Milo. The facts of the case are of a nature that raises questions about how it ever got to the Fair Work Commission.

Coles provided distribution centre employees with free Milo for drink breaks. Gary Homes liked to make up his own mix of Milo, drinking chocolate, coffee and raw sugar, which he blended at home and brought to work in a Tupperware container. He also brought a thermos of hot water to put into his mix at work. Another employee alerted management; three senior managers investigated and found Homes guilty of theft. His offence was to take Coles' property, the tin of Milo, to his home to make his mix.

The Fair Work Commission found that sacking Homes was disproportionately harsh. 'Mr Homes' behaviour could not be properly characterised as theft. The matter could have been addressed through instruction and certainly did not strike at the very heart of the employment relationship,' it concluded.

Coles also asserted that Homes had threatened his acting operations manager, Craig Snoad, in response to his sacking. It is hard to imagine a sane person taking the news well that he had been sacked from a six-year job for stealing a few scoops of Milo. After telling Homes he was sacked, Snoad said he would escort him from the premises. Homes, who thought Snoad was 'two-faced', responded, 'If I see you out on the street don't try to talk to me.'

'I'll write that down,' Snoad said.

'Good,' Homes said, 'because you might forget.'

The commission rejected Coles' argument that this exchange constituted a threat, and ordered Homes to be reinstated and paid five months' wages.

The majority of court cases involving Coles and Woolworths are 'slip-fall' matters. There is no doubt that the supermarkets take safety seriously. Woolworths even produces a DVD, poster and fact sheet for staff during grape season 'to raise awareness of the hazards of grapes on the store floor resulting in a significant reduction in customer falls from slipping on grapes'. The company has a 'Destination Zero' policy on accidents and an education policy called 'Keeping Safety Fresh'. Such attention, which Coles also applies, has grown out of hard experience. But when safety has been compromised, this attention has not stopped the supermarkets from being zealously litigious, against both their employees and their customers.

In the 2013 case of Jack Nicolaides, a Coles store assistant at Doncaster East, in Melbourne, Coles argued that when Nicolaides slipped and broke his wrist in a loading dock while leaving work to go to his car, he was not injured 'in the course of his employment', because Coles did not own the loading dock itself. It was an absurd distinction, the Victorian County Court found, as the employee could not leave his job other than via the loading dock. Coles lost again.

No case has been too small for legal contest, and the supermarkets are of course entitled to protect their rights. A by-product of Coles' and Woolworths' legal persistence has, however, been the exposure of some disconcerting in-store procedures.

Teresa Bourchdan was sacked from her position on the checkout at Coles in Merrylands, Sydney, on 19 May 2008 for breaching the employees' code of conduct. She had worked there for six years, on shifts from five pm to midnight, five nights a week, for $420, or $84 per shift. She admitted she commonly took packets of cigarettes off shelves and put them aside at a service desk with the intention of paying for them later, either for herself or for her co-workers. Coles argued that this, a normal practice among staff, breached the employee code.

What was interesting was the extent to which Coles would prosecute Bourchdan. In the Fair Work Commission hearing in 2009, several practices emerged. For evidence, Coles had used CCTV footage against its own employees. 'Statements' were produced from Bourchdan and other employees that were not signed or dated, and were all in the same handwriting. The implication was that Coles had improperly produced them. Bourchdan had never been served with a warning. Her store manager dismissed her without giving a reason, and sent her to a meeting with investigators in Chullora. There, Bourchdan was told she was not being sacked for stealing but rather for allowing other workers to take cigarettes through her checkout without paying for them. At a meeting with her regional manager, Cathleen Scarce, Bourchdan 'begged for another opportunity'. 'Why,' she asked, 'would I risk my job for a lousy packet of cigarettes?' And why would Coles later pursue the matter through an expensive appeals process in the courts, even though Coles' own report on Bourchdan noted that she 'appears to be a genuine, hard working individual who was by her own account and that of her supervisors a loyal employee. She strongly denies ever stealing any of the company's stock and it has to be said that she gave a credible defence of her actions.'

The reason Coles had the CCTV footage of Bourchdan was perhaps even more troubling. Believing a customer was stealing cigarettes, the company was, in the words of Steve Woods, a Coles Asset Protection officer, staging a 'covert operation.' It was during the course of this surveillance that 'other issues at the Merrylands store' arose. In other words, while spying on customers, Coles ended up spying on employees.

After her sacking, Bourchdan suffered from anxiety and depression. The Fair Work Commission found in her favour, and Coles was ordered to keep paying her wage until she found new employment. Coles appealed, but lost; the commission found that the dismissal of a loyal employee was not a reasonable response to the unproven suspicion that she had sneaked free cigarettes through her checkout for fellow employees.

Surveillance of employees has elsewhere provided the supermarkets with evidence to dismiss them. Allan Robinson, a forklift driver for Woolworths in Brisbane, was sacked on 21 July 2011 for 'serious misconduct': he did not 'scan off' electronically before a toilet break. Evidence before Fair Work Australia showed that the 'Woolworths

Management System', an electronic monitoring system in its distribution centres, used ostensibly to measure productivity, also surveilled employees' movements. The technology that was meant to measure Robinson's output with his forklift truck was instead used to spy on him. FWA ordered the reinstatement of Robinson and chided Woolworths for its practices.

Just as no breach would be too small, no employee is loyal enough. Robinson had worked for Woolworths for nineteen and a half years. Helen Lawrie had worked in administration for Coles for twenty-six years in Port Pirie, South Australia, when the store manager, Tory Annese, told her in 2006 that her job was being restructured out, and 'the only job we've got left for you is on check-outs'. Lawrie told Annese that osteoarthritis in both ankles made standing up to work for entire shifts impossible for her. Coles ignored her medical certificates and rostered her on checkout duty. Lawrie took her annual and long-service leave, hoping that when she returned to the store another clerical job might be found.

During this time, as she was a member of the SDA, Lawrie asked a union official, Geoff Buckland, to represent her in meetings with the supermarket. Not liking this approach, Coles asked Lawrie why she had gone to the union rather than appealing personally through the levels of management. Lawrie replied that she 'had seen people go to Area Managers or to Human Relations with problems, but this achieved nothing as Area Managers and Human

Relations seemed to agree with Management all the time'.

The South Australian Industrial Relations Court found that Coles had evaded its obligation to offer Lawrie a reasonable alternative job or redundancy. It ordered Coles to pay her $18,275, or six months' salary, the paltry amount which the multibillion-dollar company had gone to the court to challenge.

So much for how the supermarkets have dealt with their own people. For legal doggedness, both companies have outdone themselves in pursuing their customers.

In 2008 Maria Haleluka, a 48-year-old nurse, foster carer and breast cancer sufferer, was squatting to look at items on a low shelf in an aisle in a Coles supermarket in Kellyville, Sydney, when an employee pushed a fully laden dairy trolley into her, injuring Haleluka's right hip and lower back. The District Court ordered Coles to pay her $497,000. Coles denied all liability and alleged contributory negligence on Haleluka's part. Although Coles set private investigators on her trail and produced covert video footage of her, the court found 'little basis' for Coles' arguments that she was exaggerating her injury. Coles appealed to the Supreme Court, and lost there too.

Haleluka's case is one of a long list of expensive attempts by the supermarkets to evade or minimise their responsibilities to injured customers. Very often, they have used the legal system to obstruct or pursue the weak.

Philip Clarke was a 46-year-old disabled man who walked with a stick, and was known in the Coles supermarket at Lane Cove, Sydney, to enjoy sampling fresh fruit for taste. This had been allowed as a harmless practice; it's hard to imagine spending any time in a supermarket fresh food section without seeing someone pop something into their mouth. On 4 September 2009, however, Clarke got more than he bargained for. He bought some green prawns at the seafood counter. As Clarke stood at the checkout, the store manager, Shant Tatosian, shouted at him: 'I want you to open your pockets and show me those prawns! You are not free to go until you admit that you have stolen from Coles!' When Clarke showed that he had no concealed prawns, Tatosian accused him of having stolen and eaten the prawns raw. Police were called. Tatosian denied he had accused Clarke of stealing. In the NSW District Court, Clarke sued Coles for defamation, won and was awarded $40,000. Coles took the matter to the Court of Appeal, and lost.

No case of a supermarket victimising a weak customer is more notorious than that of Kathryn Strong and the hot chip. Strong, an amputee walking with crutches, went to Taree's Centro shopping mall on 24 September 2004 with her daughter and a friend. They were passing through an area between Woolworths and Big W when Strong leaned forward to look at some pot plants on sale. The tip of her crutch came down on a hot chip; she slipped and suffered a serious spinal injury. The NSW District Court ordered

Woolworths to pay her $580,000. Woolworths had the decision reversed in the NSW Court of Appeal, but in 2012 the High Court reinstated the original ruling against the supermarket.

Like any complex legal case, the argument turned on the arcane language of liability, negligence and causation of damage. Woolworths, as is its right, chose to pursue the matter, and defended itself when Strong took it to the highest court in the country. But in reputational terms, the publicity around the case only confirmed Australians' worst suspicions about big corporations: that they would use the legal system to intimidate the weak, in this case all over a hot chip. It was the disconnect between the size of Woolworths, the expense of the case and the pettiness of the central issue – the case pivoted around whether Woolworths could be expected to clean up that area of the floor at lunchtime every fifteen minutes or every twenty minutes – that left the public asking whether the supermarket giant had lost touch with reality.

The Strong case would have been an embarrassment for Woolworths whether it won or lost; the fact that it lost only sharpened the appearance of a diminished sense of proportion. But the supermarkets have not always failed in court. Coles defended a Victorian case for ten years after a customer, Melissa Roch, alleged that she was assaulted by security guards in a supermarket in Footscray, in Melbourne's west. Coles successfully avoided liability, not because it could prove the assault had not happened but because the security company was a contractor which no longer existed; it was not, therefore, Coles' problem. In 2009 Coles won an appeal against an order to pay $298,000 to a customer, Rebecca Tormey, who had been injured by a trolley pushed into her by two young male customers at its supermarket in Gladesville, Sydney. The District Court had found that by not stopping the rowdy boys, Coles bore responsibility for Tormey's injury, but the NSW Court of Appeal found that Coles did not have enough staff in the Gladesville store to know about the rowdy men, and therefore that the supermarket was not negligent.

It is inevitable that businesses that employ 400,000 people and serve half of Australia will find themselves in disputes. How the supermarkets decide to pursue these disputes, legally, is assessed internally. Whether the benefits have outweighed the costs is for the companies to judge. But the damage Coles and Woolworths have done to their reputations by marshalling their resources in the courts is beyond calculation, even when they win.

What do these disputes, collectively, tell us – aside from affirming the truism that organisations with massive financial resources tend to assert, at law, a bottomless stock of righteousness? The supermarkets' opponents in court, if analysed as a group, have one common factor: they are society's weak. Kathryn Strong was a Taree amputee. Philip Clarke was on a disability pension. Maria Haleluka was a breast cancer sufferer and foster carer. Melissa Roch and Rebecca Tormey were young middle-class mothers. Helen Lawrie, Allan Robinson, Teresa Bourchdan, Jack Nicolaides, Gary Homes, Ian Warfe, Barry Buckland and Mario Sisko were medium- to long-term employees on poor wages, sometimes less than $15 an hour, even after many years working for the same supermarket. As customers and employees, these people represented the supermarkets' core demographic: battling Australians. From the supermarkets' annual reports and websites, you would think these people were Coles' and Woolworths' pride and joy. But in the aisles and storage rooms, on the checkouts and in the loading bays, a different picture emerges.

In this light, we can reinterpret the supermarkets' role in Australian life. By keeping their prices down and employing untold thousands of unskilled workers, they have a massive de facto social welfare impact. People from all walks of life choose to shop at Coles and Woolworths, but pensioners and the unemployed shop there because they have no choice. Many employees are, like the kids in the Woolies ads, on their rite of passage through a first job, but many others, particularly those who stay on for years, are poorly paid and low-skilled, one step from the dole.

Coles and Woolworths contribute to social cohesion by enabling Australians on shoestring budgets to buy cheaply, and by giving them jobs. But while this may be a sincerely held tenet of the companies' mission, the experience from dispute resolution shows that, at the levels of middle and lower management, Coles and Woolworths will stand on their rights to the point of bullying the underclass. In a 2013 case Woolworths pursued one former low-paid employee, Michael Svajcer, who was claiming workers' compensation for a back injury. Its main argument was that a separate conviction for having sex with a fifteen-year-old girl showed that Svajcer could not have been genuinely injured. Woolworths won its case – but at what cost? Who were the companies really looking after, and who were they fighting?

The risk for corporations in making a big deal about 'people' – in embracing Mitt Romney's declaration that they are not machines but human beings – is that it cuts both ways. If companies want to shed the mask of abstraction and 'humanise' themselves, they must understand that they are responsible for *all* their actions towards human beings, whether staff or customers. When businesses are as big as Coles and Woolworths, it is inevitable that the idea of perfection painted in annual reports and other corporate documents is only a rough approximation of the daily reality.

Daily, weekly and monthly disputes such as those outlined in this chapter are nothing new. They have accumulated, over the years, into a stock of popular memory, which plays some part in the mood of scepticism that has settled over the public mind in relation to Coles and Woolworths. The question is: does the true 'culture' of these organisations live closer to the corporate mission or to the ugliness revealed in legal disputes? Is the truth about this 'culture' demonstrated in the hostile treatment of troublesome customers and employees in the courts, or in the high-minded statements from the top – or somewhere else? Or is it fairer to examine 'culture' through the companies' way of doing business from day to day, away from the harsh glare of messy and sometimes extreme legal disputes?

Slip-fall cases, no matter how unfairly approached, may provoke passing outrage or ridicule, but they are not the touch-paper that might set off a widespread reaction against Coles or Woolworths. Only a systematic business practice that is seen to offend Australian values will do that. In order to excite the emotions, such a practice would have to attack not an abstract stakeholder group or industry sector, but human beings like ourselves. It is here that Romney's casting of corporations as 'human beings, my friend' is most dangerous, for it may come back and hit the corporation like a boomerang. For the supermarkets, that moment began in 2011, three years into Ian McLeod's five-year plan to transform Coles.

CHAPTER 4

YANKING THE CHAIN

W hen Ian McLeod arrived at Coles in 2007, there was only so much he could do in eradicating competitors. Most of that work had already been done. Orbiting a mega-retailer are three major planets – competitors, suppliers and customers – and by the mid-2000s, Coles and Woolworths had disposed of most competitors. This gave rise to a fear that they would turn their sights on customers. 'Normally,' says former ACCC commissioner Stephen King, 'you would expect two big players to be cosy on price.'

But an ACCC inquiry into grocery prices in 2008 found that they were not rising unreasonably, if at all. Part of this was due to food price deflation amid the global financial crisis. While this was good luck, there was also a strategic reason: the supermarkets were not using their power to squeeze the customer, but were instead taking aim at those who made and distributed the goods.

This was a watershed moment in the supermarket

business. John Durkan, upon joining McLeod at Coles, observed: 'We also needed to get back to being customer facing; the company had drifted away from the core retailing principle of making sure the items customers wanted were there for them to buy, rather than just offering them what suppliers had available. In the first few weeks we held hundreds of meetings with suppliers to get feedback, and whilst they clearly wanted a resurgent, successful Coles, they had to also accept that they would have to supply what the customers wanted rather than what suited them to supply.'

This sounds very reasonable and warm, a way of putting the customer first. In fact, it was putting the retailer first. Coles had its eye on the fat margins and comfortable terms it thought its suppliers were enjoying. McLeod and his team had a genius for increasing sales and profitability at a time prices were falling. In 2011 they lowered prices by an average of 10 per cent, and Coles' revenues took off. Who was paying? Not customers, certainly. And as long as customers were paying less, we and our political representatives stopped asking the question.

Durkan was a leading member of the team that refined the 'customer facing' strategy in a project called Active Retail Collaboration, or ARC, which began in 2011. In Coles' official history, produced two years later, Durkan reflected with satisfaction: 'The tensions brought about through the pressure placed on suppliers to be more customer-facing helped to create an environment for innovation and have also prompted our competitors to lift their game as well. That's just fine from our perspective . . .' He might have spoken too soon, for, as we will see, ARC was a time bomb ticking away under the sheeny surface of Coles' increasing profits.

The strategy of shifting profit margin from supplier to retailer was by no means new. Nearly a decade before the arrival of McLeod and his Brit pack, a 1999 House of Representatives inquiry into the retail trading sector, chaired by Liberal MP Bruce Baird, described the market as 'heavily concentrated and oligopolistic in nature' and expressed concern about 'predatory pricing and unconscionable market conduct'. Of the 332 submissions to Baird's inquiry, 285 were opposed to the increasing power of Woolworths and Coles.

One area of creeping concern for the inquiry was supplier rebates. Rather than just buying products from suppliers and selling them to the public, the chains were charging their suppliers for shelf space and other advantages, or auctioning such privileges, and playing off suppliers against each other. The supplier most willing to pass profit back to the supermarket got the best space. Rebates, or 'trade spend' – a term embracing a fast-growing array of new ideas of how to monetise shelf space – were to be the vehicle for a multibillion-dollar transfer of wealth from food manufacturers to food retailers.

Rebates had been pioneered in the United States, refined in the United Kingdom and imported into Australia.

David Jones and Myer had been criticised for sending suppliers to the wall by ramping up rebates in the 1990s. In the 2000s Coles and Woolworths were to take the practice, as ever, to an industrial scale.

How do rebates work? Here's an example. Consumer psychologists had found that shoppers tended to move around the circumference of supermarkets, ducking into the aisles while passing. Therefore, the ends of aisles were a prized position: if your items were at an end, they would be seen by all shoppers, not just those going up that aisle. Likewise, shoppers were found to spend more time looking at items on certain shelves. The retailers decided to charge suppliers for these spaces, or make them bid against each other, as if shelf space were real estate; the loser was pushed out, or over the 'cliff', ceding its position; the practice became known as 'cliffing'.

In another example of trade spend, suppliers were also asked to pay 'voluntary' marketing kick-ins. When the supermarket started a new advertising campaign, it told the suppliers that it wasn't only advertising itself, but also them and their products. So, it argued, the advertising costs should be shared. It was entitled to hold this view, but what caused concern were the measures it took to pressure suppliers to agree.

It was already known in 1999 that if suppliers did not comply with the supermarkets' wishes, they were faced with threats such as 'range reviews', in which the retailers would establish whether or not suppliers had met 'hurdle rates' of sales. If they hadn't, they were often displaced by supermarket private brands. When McLeod came to Coles, he became a champion of private brands. In his time, private-brand sales doubled as Coles vertically integrated retail with production.

Up until then, the packaging of private-brand goods had not resembled that of independent brands. They were a cheap option, not in direct competition with branded products, but sold to appeal to customers for whom a low price was the only issue. Now, under the McLeod regime, the plain red-and-white packaging of Coles home brands was thrown over, and the labels now looked suspiciously like those of the products with which they were in competition. The very presence of the in-house brands on the shelves placed pressure on the outside suppliers, who knew that if they did not cough up for the best space, it would be taken by private-brand items that no longer looked like the down-market option.

Confronted by Coles' turnaround, Woolworths was on the same trail with its 'Woolworths Select' brands. In 2011 its board appointed a new managing director and CEO, Grant O'Brien, with a specific brief to counter Coles, which had blossomed during McLeod's three and a half years. To carve out customer loyalty and defeat the 'Colesworths' impression – a weakness of the copycat history was that 84 per cent of customers weren't loyal to either Coles or Woolies – O'Brien directed a strategy to mine customer data and strengthen a loyalty program in association with

Qantas. It was touted as a rare breakaway from Coles, even if Woolworths, too, was following what Tesco and others had done in the United Kingdom.

Under McLeod's five-year plan, meanwhile, Coles' revenues were on the way to overtaking Woolworths'. Having established the 'customer-facing' outlook Wesfarmers wanted, McLeod intensified the attack on what Coles still saw as a too costly supply chain. In January 2011, now the 'customer's friend' after its strategy of driving down prices, Coles turned to the customer's number one staple: milk. But it was a risk. 'Improving efficiencies in the supply chain' sounds impersonal, and if suppliers are big multinationals, most consumers will think, *Better them than us*. 'Suppliers' remains an abstract concept. But when the suppliers are seen as Australian farmers with dirt under their fingernails, and if those farmers start saying that food production and security in this country is being compromised, then customers might begin to wonder whether the suppliers are not 'them', in fact, but us.

After sixteen years as a dairy farmer, in January 2015 Mike Blacklock packed it in. His farm of 200 milking cows at Moorland, on the lush paddocks of the Manning River delta, on the mid-north coast of New South Wales, produced 1.3 million litres a year. Blacklock had survived the traumatic, small-farm-killing deregulation of the dairy industry in 2001, only to find a new kind of regulation taking its place. 'The constraints on our income are absolute,' he says. 'There is market domination by the supermarkets. They control the show.'

Senator Nick Xenophon, a rare voice in Canberra speaking on behalf of food suppliers and against Woolworths and Coles, says farmers such as Blacklock are 'collateral damage from the milk price war between the supermarkets'.

In 1999, when Blacklock started farming, Coles and Woolworths were buying 25 per cent of Australia's fresh milk. After deregulation in 2001, when regional supply arrangements and prices were unlocked, the supermarkets' share doubled. Initially, Blacklock sold his milk to the Gerringong and Dairy Farmers cooperatives, but switched in 2009 to Norco, which has the contract to supply Coles' own-brand milk in the northern half of New South Wales.

On Australia Day 2011, Coles launched its one-dollar own-brand milk campaign, the leading edge of its 'Down Down' marketing push. This was the apotheosis of Ian McLeod's tenure at Coles. Woolworths soon followed the one-dollar milk strategy, which was not, of course, about selling milk, but rather aimed to attract foot traffic to stores. Consumers would inevitably pick up other items as they went to and from the dairy section, which was located far from the checkouts.

Coles was ramping up its attack on suppliers' margins, but this time the supplier was the long-suffering, plain-speaking Australian dairy farmer, who was not backward in coming forward and saying how the changes were hurting him. The one-dollar milk campaign 're-duced the amount sold at a premium price, so more was sold at home-brand price by Norco', Blacklock says. 'It constrained what Norco could pay us.'

The pressure from the milk war rippled outwards. Processors of branded milk, such as the multinationals Lion and Parmalat, found that their biggest customer was now their toughest competitor, through private-brand milks that wore labels that increasingly resembled those of their Dairy Farmers, Pura or Pauls brands. They were loath to challenge the supermarkets for violation of intel-lectual property. 'It's not a good look if you take your big-gest customer to court,' an executive from one of the processors says.

Out in the countryside, meanwhile, dairy farmers who were not selling to a Coles- or Woolies-aligned pro-cessor feared a wipe-out. Non-supermarket retailers who relied on selling milk saw their custom fall. The campaign also shut down the possibility of alternative buyers. The supermarkets, including IGA and Aldi, buy and sell ap-proximately 53 per cent of Australia's fresh milk, but the retailers who sold the other 47 per cent – thousands of tiny corner stores, convenience stores and service sta-tions – were not suddenly lining up to buy from the pro-cessors. 'The one-dollar milk campaign capped the whole market,' says the processor's executive. 'Small shops would go and buy their milk at Coles or Woolies and then stock it themselves.'

Coles and Woolworths intended the processors to take the heat of the cost-cutting. But there were limits to how low the processors could go. 'Milk is a resource-intensive, expensive supply chain,' the executive says. 'There's a lot of cost in refrigeration and transport: tankers from the farm to the processor, chilled trucks to every store, large and small. The demand on quality is high.'

Soon, at the dairy farmer's end, the pain was felt. 'Coles and Woolworths picked their processors on price,' Blacklock says. 'They control the advertising, the price between home brand and branded products. Processors also had to pay for shelf space and position. When they're cutting prices, the processors skim their margins as hard as they can. Eventually, that's us farmers paying. We are at the bottom of the chain.'

Milk hit a nerve that ached far beyond the dairy industry. Most people need milk and would prefer to pay less for it, but while there may not be great public sympathy for the processors, few wanted to hurt the honest dairy farmer. Coles faced an ACCC investigation for predatory pricing on milk, and was told it could continue discounting but not to the point that it was losing money. The supermarket's public relations ascendancy was slipping away. When Coles produced a social media animation showing farmers receiving higher prices after the milk war, the ACCC forced it to withdraw it as misleading.

Public concern led the Senate to hold an inquiry – titled 'Milking it for all it's worth' – which recommended stronger measures to protect suppliers from supermarket domination. But while the politicians listened to interested parties and made recommendations, the supermarkets' attack on the supply chain continued apace as Woolworths joined the discounting race. Mike Logan, CEO of Dairy Connect, the body representing dairy farmers in New South Wales, says the supermarkets continued placing 'an artificial ceiling on price. Milk is not worth a dollar a litre, but that was a decision made by supermarket executives. The ACCC told them they couldn't lose money on milk, so to keep those discounts going they could only pass their costs on to suppliers.'

Some farmers, tired of their subordinate position as price-takers, saw an opportunity to take more control. The so-called 'Woolworths Seven' in northern New South Wales approached Woolworths directly in 2013, and contracted to supply milk to the supermarket rather than to the processor, Parmalat, which became their service-provider rather than their customer. 'When the Woolworths Seven approached them with this plan to get more money for their milk,' Logan recalls, 'Parmalat said, "You have no idea how hard it is to deal with Woolworths." The farmers said, "Let's find out."' The Woolworths Seven began producing 'value-added' milk, leaving the big processors to fight out the lower-margin private-brand business. The beverage giant Lion, at odds with Coles after the milk wars, disinvested in the processing business; Coles went into partnership with the Victorian cooperative Murray Goulburn to produce its own-brand milk from 1 July 2014.

What this meant for the industry, according to one of the Woolworths Seven, was that there was 'some improvement on price but the average dairy farmer's costs have gone up, so we're getting squeezed again. It's an improvement on twelve months ago on prices, but costs are outstripping them. We prefer not to see supermarkets having price wars on our product.'

That battle pushed Mike Blacklock into retirement. 'The Woolies Seven move was good for those farmers but bad for the industry. Divide and conquer is the supermarkets' game. Woolies could look like they're looking after the farmers, but they're only looking after a few, not the industry, which has taken a battering and can't fight another fight. The supermarkets are pretty clever. They don't want to destroy the industry but they want to push prices down to that point just above where they destroy it.'

The ultimate impact, he says, is a decline in farm investment and quality. 'What do we do? We don't buy new equipment, we downgrade the quality of our business through cutting costs on fertiliser and feed. We employ fewer people. We reduce repairs and maintenance. That's what is happening on most farms.'

Blacklock's departure is part of a long-term decline. Thirty years ago Australia had 30,000 dairy farms, of which 75 per cent were family-owned, employing 60,000 people. Now it has 7500 farms, the majority owned by foreign companies, employing 21,000 workers. Australia's annual milk production has fallen from 12 billion to 9 billion litres, Logan says, while New Zealand's has risen from 9 billion to 20 billion. 'How do small businesses operate in a world where two big businesses have so much power and are gouging each other's eyes out? It's offensive when your product is chucked in the bargain bin. It's emotional, a slap in the face.'

Logan's hope is that farmers will be saved by international demand and rising exports. 'I think one-dollar milk will naturally die. Farmers want to define the market, but we are not smart enough to beat Coles and Woolworths in the ACCC. Our solution is not to go to the ACCC but to find other markets, which will make Coles and Woolworths supply-constrained.'

The milk war, as part of Coles' 'Down Down' campaign, delighted Wesfarmers management and shareholders; during that period, Coles' sales overtook Woolworths' for the first time in decades. But the rumblings from suppliers – through their representative body, the Australian Food and Grocery Council (AFGC), through independent politicians such as Xenophon, and through the ACCC – were growing louder. If Coles was improving its profits while cutting prices, there had to be a large transfer happening somewhere, and it was the makers and growers of food who were paying. It was Nick Nikitaras's question – 'How expensive is that cheap product?' – writ large. If Coles and Woolworths were shifting profit from the food industry to themselves, and doing so without hurting supermarket shoppers, then the consequences would be felt somewhere else. The suppliers were claiming that disinvestment and the long-term degrading of Australian food production would be the outcome.

Durkan, who as Coles' head of merchandise was a key executive in implementing the plan, is said in Coles' official history of the period to 'refute those claims with ease'.

'It's an honour that people want to try and pick apart what we have been doing,' Durkan wrote, 'but what we're doing is not that complicated. We ask suppliers to give us what we can sell to customers and if they do that, customers will buy more of it and everybody wins. Australian milk consumption hadn't gone anywhere in ten years and now it has, which means greater production for more farmers. We started making commitments to growers so that they could invest in innovation that would improve their output and profitability. These steps are important for food sustainability in Australia, not just for suppliers.'

This is a statement with a horizon of perhaps the three to five years in which a top executive must please his board and shareholders. Farmers, and the Australian agricultural economy, have, or should have, a longer-term vision. The supermarkets' current strategy is to increase their vertical integration by entering 'long-term' contracts for own-brand milk with supplier-processors, as

Coles has done with Murray Goulburn. Coles boasts about 'up to 10-year tenure' in those contracts, but as the case of CRF in Colac, in south-western Victoria, shows, those ten years are not always what they seem, and often have a sting in their tail.

In 2001, CRF, a meatworks, became the national supplier of Coles' own-brand lamb. Under a ten-year contract, CRF would provide and package the meat in cuts and portions suitable to Coles' Australia-wide orders. (The initial deal was done for Coles by Peter Scott, who would later be sacked for taking a bribe – a home unit from supplier Tasman Meats. In those days, 'trade spend' could be more direct than bidding for better shelf space.)

For nearly a decade, the partnership was fruitful, worth $40 million to CRF, which employed 400 people and became a mainstay of life in Colac. But towards the end of the ten years, Coles began pressuring CRF to change its terms of supply, foregoing profit and increasing rebates, but without the compensating offer of a definite contract extension.

The owners of CRF put it up for sale and attracted several interested parties. Coles was one, seeing an opportunity to vertically integrate: it could own its supplier. According to one source close to the deal, Coles was 'successful with some pretty aggressive tactics making [it] the last man standing'. Coles allegedly let it be known to other bidders that if anyone else won the bid, Coles would withdraw its lamb contract from CRF. Perhaps fearing that the plant could lose its main source of business, other bidders dropped away.

Coles agreed to buy CRF for $10 million, with a three-month due diligence period. During that period, Coles raised complaints and issues for renegotiation. Knowing there were no other bidders, it talked the price down to just $3 million. But Coles had gone too far. Some of CRF's shareholders, feeling they had nothing to lose, scrabbled together a deal with a private equity company and fended Coles off. Coles duly made good on its threat and took its lamb contract away. The owners of CRF approached Woolworths, which declined to do business with them; one supermarket executive told the directors that 'supermarkets can be vindictive'.

With neither Coles nor Woolworths as a customer, CRF could not maintain the scale of its operations by selling meat in piecemeal deals to smaller retailers. The plant eventually survived by redirecting its products to large orders from the Asian export market. It was sold in 2013 to the Australian Lamb Company, which now exports 82 per cent of its meat.

Coles took its business to the largest food processor in the world, JBS Swift, a Brazilian company with a plant in Melbourne. In 2014 Coles began to heavily discount its own-brand lamb, as it had done with milk and bread.

The consequences for food production are similar

across industries. A senior executive with an east-coast meat processor has observed the same disinvestment as there has been in milk. 'When a business's margins are being squeezed, they cut capital expenditure. That's what gives. If a farm has a bad year, it stops investing in improving the soil or equipment. It can do that for a number of years, but eventually the lack of investment will tell. That's happened across the board. If you don't continue to invest, the results will be catastrophic. Importing product is the next step unless there's some regulatory or consumer backlash. It's a bleak outlook for Australian food production.'

The merits of agricultural rationalisation can be debated. But the object of deregulation and the National Competition Policy was to increase productivity through competitiveness in markets. Instead, the outcome has been to abet an incestuous competitiveness between Coles and Woolworths that has had the contradictory effect of decreasing competition by shutting others out of the ring. In milk, DairyConnect's Mike Logan says, 'There is essentially just this one fresh milk channel.'

Dee Margetts, the former Greens Senator for Western Australia, has written a PhD on the failures of the National Competition Policy with reference to dairy and retail. Margetts submitted evidence to the Harper Review, the current federal government's review of competition policy, supporting her argument that the only winners in the milk wars were the two supermarket chains. Outside Coles and Woolworths, effective market-wide competition was reduced. 'By the major supermarket chains reducing the gap between farmgate and retail prices for their homebrand milk products, instead of competing against each other, they could use their combined market power to secure even greater market dominance and destroy more of their smaller and independent retail competitors,' she concluded.

The supermarkets' standard response is that farmgate milk prices (literally, the price that goes to the farmer) are geared to global demand via the export milk price, not by retailers' discounting action. The winners, they respond, are the customers, who pay less for their milk. And that is a fair point in the immediate term, says Mike Logan – until the producers can no longer afford to stay afloat, and fewer suppliers in the hands of fewer retailers create the conditions for prices to go up again.

The supermarkets also argue that their dominance of fresh milk sales is by no means absolute. According to the farmers' peak body, Dairy Australia, supermarkets account for 53 per cent of milk sales. (This includes Aldi, which sells a private-brand milk, Farmland, supplied by Norco.) The effect of the milk wars was to increase the supermarkets' overall market share by 1.5 per cent, mainly at the expense of small convenience stores and service stations (nearly half of which are, of course, controlled by Coles and Woolworths). That still leaves a large chunk of the market outside the supermarkets' reach. The difficulty for suppliers without supermarket own-brand contracts is that the non-supermarket sector is too diffuse to be cost-effective: imagine the economic differences between having a single Coles or Woolworths contract and dealing separately with thousands of corner stores, who may prefer to buy their one-dollar milk from Coles anyway, and sell it for four. Collectivisation is the only viable strategy for dairy farmers, but once the major supermarket customers are taken out, there is no profitable large-scale target for the farmers to reach.

More damagingly, the producers argue, the milk wars changed the balance of branded versus own-brand sales *within* the supermarket sector. In 2013/14, this shift was still accelerating, with own-brand milk sales increasing by 4.9 per cent and company brand sales falling by 2.8 per cent. Since 2000, the share of own-brand milk products sold in supermarkets had risen from 25 per cent to 54 per cent. When it comes to fresh full-cream milk, by 2014 the supermarkets were selling two dollars' worth of own-brand milk for every dollar's worth of branded milk. In three years since the milk wars began, victory could be declared: Coles' and Woolworths' own brands had decimated their opposition.

In the milk wars, Coles and Woolworths were importing a US/UK template for supermarket profit growth. Strengthen the market share of own-brand milk through heavy discounting. Bring prices of branded milk down by demanding more cost-cutting and rebates from suppliers. Force suppliers, through the combined effect of discounting and beefing up own-brand presence, to accept reduced terms. Bring more customers into supermarkets for milk, and encourage them to fill their baskets with other items. And it worked. But it damaged the supermarkets' reputation at a time when they were setting up their most audacious assault on their supply chain.

The 1999 Baird inquiry had cautiously recommended an increase in the ACCC's powers to regulate 'unconscionable conduct' by dominant supermarket companies. It would be twelve years before the commission found what it believed was a smoking gun.

In March 2011, just a few weeks after starting the milk wars, Coles retained the Boston Consulting Group to advise on future directions. Within one month Coles and BCG gave middle managers a series of PowerPoint presentations on how to get more out of their suppliers. This was the Active Retail Collaboration program.

Initially, ARC divided suppliers into two groups: a 'Top 50' and 'Tail Suppliers', who would be asked to pay Coles a rebate for efficiency improvements Coles said it was making. In this version of ARC, Coles aimed to raise $30 million. The managers were schooled in a script that told them what to say when they spoke to their suppliers. If the suppliers did not want to comply, the script contained warnings of 'commercial consequences', which were as yet unspecified. A trial was undertaken on three of the Top 50 suppliers: General Mills, Procter & Gamble and Nestle. Although it aimed higher, Coles was only able to negotiate rebates of 0.45 per cent of sales from Procter & Gamble, 0.6 per cent from General Mills, and nothing at all from Nestle.

Meanwhile, a trial of Tail Suppliers was attempted on the energy drink maker Red Bull. At a meeting with Red Bull on 19 August 2011, Coles managers Simon Gillies and Philip Armstrong claimed that they had cut $400,000 from the energy drink company's supply cost. In return, they sought a $200,000 rebate. The difference between the amount asked of the Top 50 and of the Tail Suppliers was, of course, not disclosed. Red Bull's representatives asked how Coles had arrived at its figures. Gillies and Armstrong, following their script, did not provide substantiation. Over the next two weeks, Red Bull's Sam Mostapha emailed Gillies and Armstrong under the subject lines 'ARC' and 'Red Bull and ARC'. Red Bull was refusing to pay the rebate; Mostapha had calculated that Red Bull's *total* costs in supplying Coles did not even come to $400,000.

Although the trials had been mismanaged, Coles pressed ahead under its key divisional managers, British executives brought in under Ian McLeod's tenure: George Dymond, head of Grocery and Food, who had served with Durkan at Carphone Warehouse, and Richard Pearson, a former first-class cricketer and Asda executive who now headed Grocery and Frozen. Dymond and Pearson reported to Durkan. This hierarchical tree was essential to what the ACCC later alleged was unconscionable bullying of suppliers.

From July through October 2011, Coles ran an 'ARC Supply Chain Boot-camp' for its category managers, with the subtitle 'Good to GREAT end to end'. The second iteration of ARC refined the supplier designation from two to three tiers. Tier 3 included 220 smaller suppliers, for whose businesses Coles constituted a 'very significant' part – at least 30 per cent. They were therefore in the weakest bargaining position. Losing the Coles account would be calamitous. From them, Coles sought an across-the-board 1 per cent rebate, aiming to raise $16 million.

Coles' category managers were trained to approach the suppliers with what were called 'ask' scripts, telling them exactly how to phrase their requests and how to respond to questions. There would be no negotiation on the rebate amount. The suppliers would be asked to consent within days. There would be no substantiation of the nature of the savings Coles was claiming. Successful category managers would become eligible for 'prizes'. If suppliers did not pay, the category managers were authorised to 'escalate' the matter to their 'Business Category Manager', who was likewise authorised to escalate it to Dymond and Pearson, even to Durkan himself. The 'commercial consequences' of non-payment included an end to supply contracts, an instant 'range review' of current products, an end to data-sharing agreements or all of the above. Range reviews at the end of a contract period were standard. Range reviews conducted amid a contract period were tantamount to a threat to renegotiate downwards.

The category managers started making the calls on 17 October 2011, and the mayhem was immediate. Within four days, three suppliers – Oates, Scalzo and Stuart Alexander – were escalated to higher managers for refusal to pay. A week later, at least twenty-five suppliers, including Dulux, Mirabella and Yakult, joined them. Within five weeks, at least sixty-two suppliers had been escalated.

Coles' response was brutal, according to the ACCC's statement of claim in the Federal Court. In response to Austech, an automotive toolmaker not paying the demanded rebate, the supermarket threatened to cut orders within two days. For Stuart Alexander, which imports brands such as Tabasco sauce, Guylian chocolates and Mentos lollies, Coles cancelled planning and promotion schedules and would not discuss whether or not they would order again. To Oates, which makes cleaning products, Coles said it would conduct a range review without consultation. Range reviews were seen as especially punitive, because, in one food producer's wry words, 'you don't hear a lot of stories about range reviews ending up with better terms for suppliers'. A storm of emails between Coles and its suppliers ensued; many of these emails would eventually fall into the ACCC's hands.

Eventually, all but thirty-two of the suppliers paid up. As the ACCC investigated the ARC scheme over the next two years, it hit a wall. The suppliers were so scared of retribution from Coles that they did not volunteer information; the commission had to use its coercive powers to obtain evidence. When the matter arrived in the Federal Court in Melbourne in June 2014, Coles said it would 'vigorously defend' its actions, saying that the ARC program was voluntary and that the company did not cut suppliers off, even the thirty-two who had ultimately refused to pay. It claimed that it did substantiate how its data-sharing and 'economic ordering' systems would save the suppliers money. It denied issuing threats, although it admitted supplying the scripts that contained details of 'commercial consequences' and 'escalation'. It made ninety-eight admissions, such as proposing not to discuss new product development with Stuart Alexander, not sharing data with Austech and limiting future sales orders unless the suppliers paid. While it maintained that the ARC program was 'at all times voluntary', Coles also admitted to rejecting Stuart Alexander's offer to pay a levy of 0.42 per cent.

Tier 3 suppliers included the Gourmet Food group, suppliers of the Rosella and Waterwheel brands, and Unibic, makers of Anzac biscuits. Both companies fell into receivership after the ARC push, if not entirely because of it. Ferrier Hodgson, the receiver of Gourmet Food, stated that the company's collapse stemmed from the trade spend demanded by the supermarkets and the competition from Coles' and Woolworths' own brands. The South Australian food company Spring Gully was one of the escalated Tier 3 suppliers; it collapsed, owing $3 million, eighteen months later. It is unclear how much of the trade spend for these companies stemmed specifically from the ARC program, but Coles may have to reimburse as much as $16 million to those suppliers who did pay up under ARC.

Why did the suppliers not simply take their business elsewhere? If the answer isn't obvious enough, it's not hard to find a cautionary tale. Food manufacturer Tony Lutfi's Greenwheat Freekeh grain product was deleted from Coles' shelves after he supplied it to other retailers in the mid-2000s. Lutfi had grown frustrated because Coles had frozen the price it paid him for eight years, and when he did not pay rebates, his product was moved to shelves where his customers could not find it. 'We told Coles and Woolworths to take a hike,' he says. 'If you can help it, they should not be the focus of any business. I don't blame them for acting in self-interest, though. It's the Australian people and their governments that have allowed them to gain that overwhelming power.'

When the ACCC launched its case against Coles in May 2014, it was sending a strong signal of resistance to that power. Its chairman, Rod Sims, said of ARC: 'These were seriously large demands, put on these companies with threats. If these allegations are proven true, that is not the sort of behaviour you want in Australian business. It's corrosive, we believe, of the effective working of a market economy.'

The exposure of even the admitted behaviour damaged Coles' reputation. 'It's a critical case,' says Gary Dawson, director of the AFGC. 'You can't overstate its importance. It could redefine what unconscionable conduct is in our sector. Even by being brought to the court it has had a positive effect.'

Over the past decade, trade spend has become central to both supermarket companies' strategies, as it has to those of retailers around the world. In Australia, according to the AFGC, trade spend now accounts for more than $4 billion, or 25.6 per cent of grocery suppliers' sales – and for large suppliers it is as high as 75.6 per cent. That means that for every dollar's worth of goods the suppliers sell, they pay back 25 to 75 cents to the supermarkets. It has been enough to wipe out all profit growth and put some into the red. According to a recent AFGC/KPMG report, trade spend is 'the major driver of the decline' in the food manufacturing business. While supermarket profits have risen at a rate of about 4 per cent a year for the past decade, suppliers' profits have flat-lined. In 2012/13, both Coles and Woolworths increased their margins through rebates, transferring about $1.5 billion to their bottom line. The less suppliers deal with Coles and Woolworths, the less their trade spend. The exposure of the trade spend Woolworths was seeking from fruit and vegetable growers for its Jamie Oliver campaign shone further light on the supermarkets' tactics.

By 2014, when the ARC program finally exploded in Coles' face, the supermarket argued that, as a sign of its willingness to play fair, it had agreed to a code of conduct in November 2013. Initiated by the AFGC, the code, by proscribing certain actions, also revealed what was believed to have been taking place. Coles and Woolworths promised not to charge (or to stop charging) suppliers for:

- 'Shrinkage' and 'wastage' of products once they were in the supermarkets' possession;
- Additional shelf space and prominent positioning;
- Listing products in their advertising; or
- Most of the cost of marketing campaigns, often without consultation.

They also agreed not to:

- Vary supply agreements unilaterally and retrospectively;
- De-list products without consultation; or
- Over-order products at a 'promotional' price and then sell them at full price, pocketing the difference.

On the issue of private brands, the supermarkets agreed not to:

- Copy brands' packaging for own-brand products;
- Appropriate brands' confidential information on product development to develop their own-brand products; or

- Replace branded products with own-brand products in the best shelf space without notice or consultation.

It was a damning document. No matter how much Coles and Woolworths denied they had been engaging in such practices, the fact that they were in the code of conduct was indictment enough, like a list of parole conditions. But the code was also voluntary. While Dawson is confident that 'a breach of the code is a breach of the [Competition and Consumer] Act', a more sceptical ACCC has voiced concerns that the supermarkets can use their market power to bind suppliers to contracts that sidestep or override the code. Nick Xenophon says the code 'has little effect because it is not mandatory; it does not [give authorities] the power to break the companies up'. The supermarkets refused to sign any AFGC code if it was mandatory. By March 2015, Coles, Woolworths and Aldi had signed the code, while Metcash 'commended' it but would trial it for twelve months before signing.

The ACCC says it is monitoring Woolworths and Metcash in the way it did Coles, which in turn will be closely watched as it approaches its next frontier: its struggling liquor business. At a Wesfarmers strategy meeting in May 2014, Durkan implied that Coles would be employing the same tactics in liquor that had worked so successfully in supermarkets. Approximately 77 per cent of Australian wine sales now go through Coles or Woolworths outlets, according to a study by the Winemakers' Federation of

Australia, and the industry is braced for the squeeze.

It has already started. The nitty-gritty of how suppliers are treated is illustrated by Brad Wehr, a West Australian vigneron with twenty-five years' experience, who says he was subjected to harsh tactics by the Woolworths-owned Dan Murphy's chain after he won an award at a 2009 wine show. 'Part of the award was that they would buy a certain volume from you,' Wehr says. 'It was a painful paperwork process but I went along with it. I felt that you needed to embrace these groups if you wanted to sell a lot of wine, because they dominate retail.'

The agreed amount was for Dan Murphy's to sell 100 cases of the prize-winning Wine By Brad. A Woolworths buyer told Wehr the chain would buy a trial supply of five cases, but sell it at a discount of between 15 and 20 per cent.

'I said I had to protect my price points because my other customers wouldn't be happy if they saw my wine cheaper elsewhere,' Wehr says. 'Woolies said that that's none of my business. The gist was, "We'll do what we like." If they saw it cheaper anywhere else, they would bargain-bin it or advertise it at $9.99. It shows the arrogance that comes with that much power.' In the end, Wehr says, he and Woolworths 'agreed that we didn't really want to do business with each other'.

Woolworths' and Coles' liquor chains have driven their own-brand wines as hard as groceries, and private-brand wines – subtly disguised – now occupy prime shelf space in Dan Murphy's and Vintage Cellars. Sarah Collingwood, a South Australian winemaker, was at a Women in Wine industry event in Adelaide in 2010 when, she says, 'it kept coming up that the supermarkets had a lot of power in the industry on the back of the labels like Cow Bombie that you can't tell have been made by them'. Collingwood developed a website – whomakesmywine.com.au – that publicised the supermarkets' own-brand wines. 'I was really surprised by how many brands they have. There are geographic themes, geological themes, cute critter themes and so on. I've never seen a Black & Gold chardonnay!'

Small producers, Collingwood says, are dismayed by 'the prospect of more and more Dan Murphy's and First Choice shelves being filled by private brands. We just want people to be able to make an informed choice'. The cost, for a supplier, is all or nothing. Collingwood's company, Four Winds, does not sell to the supermarket companies and, she says, probably never will. 'We've shot ourselves in the foot if we want to go into the retail chains. I don't think they'd forgive us.'

Of the process of attacking supply chain costs, Durkan has written: 'There were speed bumps along that road, but we just kept coming back to the same mantra: do what is right for the customer.' In the ACCC case against Coles' ARC program, the speed bumps, small and large, were to get their day in court. In early hearings Coles denied that it had been in breach of the law. Outside the court on 17 October 2014, Ian McLeod, by then in a headquarters position at Wesfarmers (he would leave the company, for the American supermarket giant Bi-Lo, in January 2015), said: 'In terms of the core charge here, I believe we will be vindicated.' McLeod said there was 'no systemic issue with Coles in relation to the way we deal with our suppliers ethically', that the ARC program comprised 'normal topics for business discussions', and that the company was regarded as 'one of the better retailers to deal with, not one of the worst'.

In its public relations battle during the court case, Coles offered journalists briefings with its legal representatives. The gist of these briefings, consistent with McLeod's speech and the company's presentations in court, was that Coles' ARC program was nothing out of the ordinary, that it was in line with supplier relations as conducted down the years in a period of increasing pressure on prices, and that it was no worse than the conduct of other supermarkets. Coles seemed to be throwing up its hands and asking, 'What have we done that is not standard practice?' It also argued that the great majority of the suppliers targeted by the ARC program in 2011 were still supplying Coles in 2014.

On the matter of their practices being standard for the industry, Coles could point, in February 2015, for instance, to wholesalers Fasttrack Logistics and Cofco Distributors lodging a Federal Court statement of claim against Metcash, which, it said, failed to take deliveries of groceries and took some $12 million in rebates, some of which was used to pay for 'study tours' for Metcash staff to Japan, Hawaii and the United States. Metcash would defend the claim that it had acted unfairly and in bad faith to damage the wholesalers' businesses.

In the early 2000s, Woolworths, in a court case unrelated to the issue, gave details of a similar program it was running. Its 'Project Mercury' came to light in an employment law matter in the New South Wales Supreme Court, brought in 2004 by a former senior manager, Mark Konrad Olson. Olson, whose title was Business Manager – Rebuying (StockSMART 1), had resigned from Woolworths in July 2004.

In February of that year, Olson had been demoted after the discovery of pornographic emails in a widespread internal scandal. Olson had worked for Woolworths since 1985, steadily climbing the corporate ladder, and the company conceded that he had been hard-working and competent before the email scandal. Since 2002 Olson had been working on Project Mercury, an endeavour to reform Woolworths' computerised ordering systems; it aimed to save the company 12 to 14 per cent of its then $20 billion supply chain budget. (Mercury was part of a larger scheme, 'Project Refresh', which would, if successful, cut $6.9 billion from Woolworths' costs. The final phase, Project Galaxy, was due for completion in April 2015, at a total IT cost of approximately $100 million.)

Mercury was being spearheaded by Bernie Brookes, who would later leave Woolworths to become chief executive of Myer. Brookes had travelled widely – studying

Walmart and Giant in the United States and Tesco in the United Kingdom, in particular – and cherry-picked what he considered the most relevant and effective tactics in how they managed their logistics and supply chains. Accenture Consulting moved in and helped Woolworths design the scheme. Initially running it was Woolworths' then chief manager of supply, Michael Luscombe, who would soon be promoted to succeed Roger Corbett as CEO.

A three-stage project starting in 1999, Project Mercury bore similarities to the streamlining of orders that Coles would implement in its ARC program a decade later. Mercury, Olson told the Supreme Court, involved an 'automated store ordering system (AutoStockR). That system utilises data collected at point-of-sale. Once that data is enhanced, it will allow for future store forecast requirements, including better promotional planning information. This will also allow Woolworths to consolidate the information up the supply chain.' For example, he said, Woolworths could 'predict how many tins of Golden Circle pineapple slices will be needed by each individual store around the country in two weeks' time. This would allow for orders to be placed against Golden Circle, for delivery by either Golden Circle or Woolworths into the Brisbane Distribution Centre for on-forwarding to stores via the Woolworths' Distribution Centre network.' Suppliers would be asked to pay rebates in recognition of the savings the new system would glean.

The project was top-secret. Corbett, the Woolworths

CEO, told the court that he would sit at Project Mercury meetings and routinely give a speech to the executives present, emphasising 'the confidential nature of the work we were doing, that this was a strategic intellectual property that Woolworths was spending tens of millions of dollars to create and the confidential nature of this business of what we were doing was ahead of the market and had significant value to our competitors'. Olson's area 'was one of intense confidentiality', Corbett told the Supreme Court.

Olson was deployed to the Parramatta corporate office, overseeing StockSMART, an important component of Project Mercury, when in early 2004 Woolworths uncovered a chain of pornographic emails sent among employees. Forty-seven Woolworths staff were involved, and those who initiated the chain were sacked. For receiving six emails, Olson was demoted. As *Dilbert* creator Scott Adams has said, 'It doesn't take many people to have a bad sense of humour to get in trouble at a corporation.'

A few months later, in May 2004, the independent supermarket chain Franklins approached Olson, offering a job similar to the one from which he had been demoted, to modernise and streamline Franklins' supply chain. Olson wasn't sure he wanted to leave Woolworths. He hoped he would be restored to Project Mercury, and met Brookes soon after his encounter with the Franklins managers. Brookes told him, 'I'm sure that your penance will be coming to an end at some stage soon,' and outlined several possible future roles for Olson back within

Mercury. Later offers did not satisfy Olson's hopes, however, and he accepted a position with Franklins.

His exit was proceeding amicably until Woolworths discovered that he had emailed confidential material about Project Mercury to his wife, and later downloaded that material to his home computer. Woolworths decided to dismiss him immediately and enforce a clause in his employment agreement that prevented him from working for a competitor such as Franklins for the next six months.

Woolworths' case was that Olson was planning to steal sensitive Project Mercury plans that were trade secrets and protected by copyright. Olson told the court he had sent himself the Project Mercury material at home so that he could review the future possibilities Brookes was offering him. He also argued that the non-compete clause in the employment agreement pertained to his earlier job, from which he had been demoted, and not to his current job.

Woolworths won the case against Olson, but although some commercial material in the case was kept confidential, it suffered collateral damage in that many details of Project Mercury were revealed in open court. Coles followed the case closely. While Woolworths' intent, which it achieved, was to stop Olson from taking the detail of Project Mercury to Franklins, its court action provided a road map for its competitors. This extended from 'Store Supply Chain Costs' ('from the supermarket back dock to the shelf, this includes the implementation of Perpetual Inventory stock management systems and Automated

Store reordering [AutostockR] and the introduction of "One Touch" stock movement initiatives such as Roll cages family grouped by store layout, store ready Unit Load Devices for selected products and store ready tray filling') through to the location and functions of distribution centres, transport management, replenishment and stock movement. The finer details might have been kept confidential, but the architecture of Woolworths' new system was laid bare. Even some of the nomenclature of Project Mercury would later be adopted by Coles almost word for word; for example, Mercury's alias, 'End to End Supply Chain Improvement', became at Coles 'Good to Great End to End'.

But Woolworths still had the jump on its competitors. Project Mercury achieved most of the savings it targeted, and was succeeded in 2014 by 'Mercury Two'. Under this refinement, Woolworths purchased 50 per cent of Quantium, a data firm that would analyse customer buying patterns in sophisticated ways, telling Woolworths not only what customers were buying, but also anticipating when and what they would buy next. It added Ezibuy, a New Zealand company specialising in online direct selling. The goal was to extend the supply chain improvements from food to other products, so that, for instance, customers could order clothes from Big W, food from Woolworths and liquor from Dan Murphy's, and then pick up everything from, say, a Masters hardware store. Eyeing the next frontier – that elusive consumer loyalty – Woolworths was trying to build a large tent of different types of retail into which to bring its customers.

Amid its ACCC case in 2014, Coles' cries of 'unfair' had to be placed in this context. The company believed it was being prosecuted for actions that it considered industry normality, and that it believed its competitors had been doing as well, from an earlier date and without being caught. That said, there was no evidence that Project Mercury included 'ask' scripts that posited 'commercial consequences' for non-compliant suppliers, and no evidence that Woolworths managers were told not to provide substantiation for the savings they were claiming.

At hearings in October 2014, the ACCC expanded its case against Coles by making specific allegations about the company's dealings with Oates and the food suppliers Benny's Confectionery and Bayview Seafoods. The new allegations were not specifically based on the ARC program but were said to typify Coles' routine dealings with suppliers. The complaints from five suppliers, including the three above, arose out of the ACCC's inquiries relating to ARC.

According to the ACCC's new case, when Coles found 'gaps' between its expected and real profits on the suppliers' products, it forced the suppliers to pay the difference, on what it called, without any apparent sense of humour, 'Perfect Profit Days'. The ACCC also alleged that Coles forced the suppliers to pay for the cost of wastage and markdowns, even when these were decisions Coles had made unilaterally, and that it fined suppliers for late deliveries without justifying the cost. On one occasion Coles allegedly demanded Oates pay it $326,590 for its 'gap', a figure Coles did not justify and which Oates refused to pay. Coles then deducted $246,400 from its next payment to Oates. When Coles indicated it would 'range review' Oates' product lines, the supplier agreed to pay the supermarket $365,200.

Jeff Kennett, who was appointed 'independent arbiter' of suppliers by Coles in August 2014, said: 'These are things that happened three years ago. I would imagine that would have been under a different administration at Coles.' The head of the relevant section at Coles in 2011 was, however, Durkan, now the company's managing director.

In some ways, the ACCC–Coles cases are a trial of reputation as much as of law. The ACCC is promoting its reputation by being seen to stand up for competition law, for consumers and, incidentally, for small food manufacturers, against a supermarket giant. While it stated it wanted to give the court 'an opportunity to consider whether conduct of this nature, if proven, is unlawful in the context of large businesses dealing with their suppliers', the commission was also making a broader point about business tactics that large sections of the public might find repugnant, whether or not they are strictly lawful.

After arguing for six months that it would 'vigorously' dispute the ACCC's case against it, in December 2014 Coles agreed to accept its punishment. It would pay $10 million in fines to the commission and $1.25 million in legal costs, but it was also facing an estimated $16 million in refunds to its suppliers. The fines were based on fifteen instances of misconduct towards eight suppliers, but the approximately 200 suppliers who paid up under the ARC program were entitled to seek compensation.

Federal Court Justice Michelle Gordon said that Coles' misconduct had been 'serious, deliberate and repeated' and 'was not done in good conscience'. 'Coles treated its suppliers in a manner not consistent with acceptable business and social standards which apply to commercial dealings,' she said. 'Coles demanded payments from suppliers to which it was not entitled by threatening harm to the suppliers that did not comply with the demand. Coles withheld money from suppliers it had no right to withhold.'

Durkan said Coles had 'crossed the line', and 'sincerely regrets and apologises for its conduct in these dealings'. He said that Coles had improved its processes with regard to suppliers since 2011.

No sooner had Coles settled with the ACCC than Woolworths came into the commission's crosshairs. Alan Ducret, the ACCC enforcement officer who had led the investigation into Coles, was examining claims that Woolworths was engaging in unconscionable conduct by demanding suppliers pay for its 'Cheap Cheap' marketing campaign. When Woolworths was reducing prices below the costs it had paid suppliers, it was going back to them to ask them to make up the difference, or 'profit fill', or else risk losing their contracts with the supermarket. A week before Christmas 2014, an unnamed sales manager for a leading health products company told Fairfax Media: 'I was asked for a contribution of almost $1 million, and when I refused to pay I was told a "range review" was under way and I would be informed of the outcome early next week. The implied threat is that some of my products will no longer be stocked if I don't pay up.' Woolworths had allegedly told suppliers that its demands had been 'endorsed' by the ACCC. The commission responded by saying it did not offer 'endorsements' of business conduct.

The reported Woolworths tactic of squeezing suppliers, called 'Operation Close the Gap', had many similarities to the 'profit fill' practices used by Coles and other supermarkets. It was led by Alex Dower, a former Tesco executive who became Woolworths' commercial director in 2012. Dower sent an email to staff in December 2014 urging them to ignore media reports about unconscionable conduct and continue what they were doing. The AFGC said that this amounted to demands from suppliers of between $70,000 and $1.5 million, with the aim of raising $50 million from them by 31 December 2014. Approximately $6.7 million had been paid by 11 December. Woolworths released a statement saying that it was doing its best to reduce prices for consumers' benefit.

Under increasing pressure from new entrants such as Aldi, and seeing threats to their future in the struggles of their model companies in the United Kingdom, Coles and Woolworths were approaching the endpoint of their campaign to squeeze suppliers. In 2014 a report by Morgan Stanley analyst Tom Keirath showed the stupendous, history-changing scale of the profit transfer Coles and Woolworths had engineered from food manufacturers to retailers. In seven years to 2014, Coles and Woolworths had increased their food profits from $2.1 billion to $4.4 billion. In four years to 2014, food suppliers' total profits had fallen from $6.1 billion to $3.7 billion. At this rate, Keirath wrote, Coles and Woolworths would be taking 100 per cent of the total profit share on food by 2020. The only force holding the supermarkets back from such domination would be action from the ACCC. But if it reaches that point, there will be nothing left to squeeze.

It's likely, however, that the supermarkets will realise they can only crunch the suppliers so far before they begin to damage themselves. There has to be an end before the destruction becomes mutual. Profit growth must come from elsewhere. As Woolworths' Mercury Two shows, the accent in the future is turning more to data and consumer behaviour, a surveillance of what we buy and when. For both supermarkets, the next holy grail requires moving the focus away from suppliers and back onto customers: they want to find ways not only of attracting our dollar, but of trapping and keeping it.

CHAPTER 5

CATCHING THE RAINBOW

T he supermarket business is increasingly a data business. Nearly everyone in Australia shops at Colesworths – not to use the term disparagingly, but as a statement of statistical truth. They use the supermarkets inter-changeably. Even though Woolworths boasts having handed out 9.8 million loyalty cards to customers, anyone who is loyal to Woolworths is probably only so because there isn't a Coles nearby. This is the problem of supermarket loyalty: there is none.

In the past, both Coles and Woolworths have made strenuous efforts to build an exclusive relationship with their customers. Loyalty cards and incentive schemes linked to frequent flyer points and other enticements have been used for more than a decade. Petrol discount dockets were an attempt to keep customers inside the Woolworths/Caltex or Coles/Shell orbit. But all that happened was that shoppers would take a both/and approach, picking up loyalty cards and petrol dockets from both chains and using them to get the lowest price at whichever service station they happened to be using. Customers were keen, all right, but promiscuously so. The supermarkets were paying the price for their decades of mimicry. Having spent so much time copying each other, they were now being treated by five in six customers as if they were one and the same.

The coming solution, or so the supermarkets would like to think, appears to lie in the links that data can reveal between shopper and supermarket. Financial services are one vehicle for building these links. Coles and Woolworths have expanded their offerings in personal loans, credit cards and insurance, and are circling financial institutions with the hint that they may even seek banking licences. Tesco, Sainsbury's and Marks & Spencer have already moved into banking in the United Kingdom, taking deposits as well as issuing loans.

While this may spook the banks, what will it mean for consumers? Coles began to offer personal loans, but not mortgages, in 2015. Its aim is to lend $800 million over the year, in partnership with finance company GE Capital. Woolworths has offered credit cards and insurance since 2009, but was prevented in 2014 from using the word 'banking' to describe any of its services; it has not announced any plans to lend money. The aim appears not to be to compete with the banks so much as to secure loyalty: to persuade consumers that there is a benefit in linking their credit cards, home and car insurance, and personal loans (in Coles' case) with their grocery, liquor, petrol, merchandise and hardware shopping. As of mid-2014, Coles Financial Services had issued 400,000 credit cards and 350,000 car, home and life insurance policies. Whether or not this succeeds – and past experience suggests that shoppers who get credit cards and insurance will continue to show loyalty only to price – it will deepen Coles' and Woolworths' knowledge of consumer patterns. Financial products may only be the means to an end. Knowledge is power, and power may lead to loyalty.

It virtually goes without saying that schemes to build loyalty had already been tried overseas. But as Coles and Woolworths mined the overseas experience ever deeper, they got a shock. Two events hit the insular world of Australian supermarkets almost simultaneously. Foreign supermarket giants noticed what rich pickings might be had in Australia, and the Tesco playbook ran out of pages.

It was in 2001 that the German chain Aldi opened its first store in Australia. (The German company is separated into two parts, Aldi North and Aldi South; it is the latter that operates in Australia.) Aldi now has more than 350 stores here, and is expanding fast. The American giant Costco also dipped its toe into Australia, but as yet only has five outlets. The German chain Lidl is set to follow.

In terms of the big picture of vertical integration and food production, Aldi, the competitor deemed most dangerous to Coles and Woolworths, is the same, only worse. Aldi's products are 95 per cent home-brand, owned by the parent, and mostly imported. A shopper wanting to support Australian food manufacturers would have to ask a lot of questions before setting foot in Aldi, which, as it operates as a limited partnership, does not file tax or financial information to the Australian corporate regulator. It claims to pay 31 per cent tax upon its profits, but this figure is not open to public analysis, and its unusual corporate structure would certainly see that those 'profits' are a minuscule fraction of Aldi's $5 billion in Australian revenues.

On the other hand, shoppers wanting to find the cheapest goods would make Aldi their first port of call. Aldi has expanded quickly into Australia by appealing to the same lowest-price, bargain-hunting instinct that has served Coles and Woolworths so well; but Aldi has taken that appeal further. In a sense, Aldi is a product and beneficiary of the 'Down Down' culture. A study by investment bank Morgan Stanley found that based on a basket of fifteen items, Aldi's own-brand products were 10 per cent cheaper than own-brand items at Coles and Woolworths. With some, the difference was found to be much greater. Blocks of Aldi cheese, at $6.00, were 20 per cent cheaper than Woolworths' own-brand cheese; canned tomatoes, at $1.18, were nearly 40 per cent cheaper.

In October 2014 Aldi announced that it planned to invest a further $700 million in this country, building two new distribution centres and another 130 stores in South Australia and Western Australia. This would bring Aldi's investment in Australia to just under $4 billion.

Significantly, this investment would come from existing Australian cash flows of $5.3 billion a year: Aldi is doing so well here that it doesn't need to draw from its German parent. Dick Smith, whose food company has supplied the major supermarkets, has forecast that in fifteen years Aldi would send Coles and Woolworths out of business. 'Both of them will go broke,' he said. 'We'll end up with two of everything – Aldi and Walmart.' Smith said that Australia 'will make Aldi boom because we're just interested in the cheapest price, but there's no doubt in my mind once they've got large market share, everything will come from China. If you think Coles and Woolies are ruthless, you wait. [Aldi] are the smartest retailers in the world.'

The threat of Aldi was dismissed by some market analysts, who predicted Coles and Woolworths would continue to increase their market share, so that Aldi's growth would come at the expense of a smaller player, such as Metcash. But Woolworths and Coles take Aldi (and Lidl) seriously because of the damage the German chains have already wrought on Tesco and the other UK supermarkets.

Tesco, historically the market leader in the United Kingdom, went on an expansion drive and a store-upgrading spree from the early 2000s, just as Aldi and Lidl moved into Britain. The timing could not have been worse. Between 1998 and 2010, Tesco's return on capital fell by one-third. Its market share fell from 30 to 28 per cent in the 2013/14 year alone. Its share price fell by 50 per cent between the end of 2011 and the middle of 2014. Meanwhile, Aldi and Lidl enjoyed double-digit revenue growth.

Compounding the fall in revenue and profit, Tesco was found to have overstated its 2013/14 profit by £250 million. The source of this error was Tesco's scheme of rebates, the template for what Coles and Woolworths have done in Australia, which were complex from an accounting point of view. There appeared to have been a timing issue over whether rebate income could be booked when the supplier contracts were agreed, when the suppliers were notified of and invoiced for their rebates, or when the rebates were paid. PwC, Tesco's auditor, had already warned in May that there was a 'risk of manipulation' in how the rebate income was reported. Initial indications were that Tesco officials had jumped the gun in reporting the income too early. Further investigations by Britain's Serious Fraud Office were looking into whether this premature action was a result of deliberate pressure or simply a mistake.

Whatever the outcome, the affair served to highlight how much stress Tesco was under. The Aldi model was cutting a swathe through British supermarkets. By stocking fewer products, bringing them into the stores in 'shelf-ready' packaging that did not need to be stacked, and by selling their own-brand goods at an average of 20 per cent cheaper than the other supermarkets, Aldi was breaking new barriers in the discounting race. Simultaneously,

Aldi in Europe and Britain had started selling a limited supply of branded goods and fresh food, expanding their lines and creeping up on the other supermarkets from the flank. Cheap, but not quite as nasty.

Tesco has been the most notable distressed supermarket in Britain, but its rivals, Sainsbury's, Asda and Marks & Spencer, have been under the same pressure. Walmart in the United States has been similarly challenged, not by Aldi so much as by the dollar stores, which amount, strategically, to the same threat. Deep discounting works. The overseas models are, as always, a guide to the future for the Australian supermarkets, but increasingly they have become not beacons of success but cautionary tales. The fear of Aldi is real, and it is to some degree energising Coles and particularly Woolworths, which is seen as the more vulnerable of the two giants, with margins of 7.43 per cent compared with Coles' 5.3 per cent. But Aldi's rise is also a political positive for the incumbents, in a roundabout way. If Woolworths and Coles are being threatened, they adduce this as evidence that there is effective competition in the supermarket sector and that they are not operating a duopoly.

Under this pressure, new growth had to be found. By the end of 2014, Coles and Woolworths were surging – simultaneously, of course – into the small convenience-store space, seeking sites of 200–400 square metres to compete with the 7-Eleven and City Convenience store brands. Commercial real estate agents reported that Coles and Woolworths had both been scouring inner-city precincts for viable sites. The Tesco playbook – now a guide to what *not* to do – had been instructive. Tesco had invested heavily in huge big-box supermarkets on the fringes of UK towns and cities. These were not doing well, as shoppers were shifting to smaller and more frequent buying trips, and increasing their online purchases; Tesco had begun trying to sell off these sites to suburban housing developers. Woolworths branded its convenience stores as 'Woolworths Small Format' in inner Sydney and Melbourne, to complement their 'Woolies Metro' medium-sized stores, with cafes built into the sites. They even made lockers available for the storage of online purchases, so that customers could come in later and pick them up.

The stores would open twenty-four hours a day, seven days a week, a continuation of the long-term relaxation of trading hours that has been benefiting Coles and Woolworths for more than two decades. A Productivity Commission report in October 2014 backed a further deregulation of trading hours, saying restrictions in retailing were out of step with contemporary consumer habits, and the Harper Review reinforced this. Woolworths managing director and CEO Grant O'Brien continues to lobby for deregulated trading hours, placing this as a number-one priority. Total deregulation is the supermarkets' aim.

Whatever the looming impact of Aldi, Costco and Lidl on the Australian supermarket giants' profits, the present was still looking rosy when financial results were posted in the second half of 2014. Woolworths' first-quarter sales for 2014/15 were $16.2 billion, an increase of 3 per cent on the previous year. O'Brien said, 'Our sales were below expectations and we didn't deliver the consistency in growth we'd been looking for,' and the results were generally disappointing to investors, but there is always a question of perspective to be applied. Like a spoilt brat, the share market is disappointed when even these mature market dominators do not produce unstoppable profit growth. O'Brien said there was no reason to downgrade the full-year forecast of a 4 to 7 per cent increase in profit. So things were not too desperate. For the quarter, food and liquor sales were up by 3.9 per cent, and even the struggling Masters hardware brand saw a 30.8 per cent increase in revenues, to $238 million, although it was still a long way from breaking even. Spearheading the supermarket division's sales growth was its recent 'Cheap Cheap' campaign, which led off by lowering the price of a loaf of own-brand bread to 85 cents. Lamb became a new sacrificial lamb, too, with aggressive price-cutting on own-brand cuts. Nonetheless, Aldi's incursions saw an alarmed share market take 18 per cent from Woolworths' share price in the year to April 2015.

Notwithstanding the disruption to their long-uninterrupted profit growth, the spread of Coles and Woolworths outlets in Australia continued apace. Woolworths opened a net nine new supermarkets in the quarter, bringing their total number to 940, while they increased their liquor presence by a further nine stores, giving Australia 1222 Woolworths-owned bottle shops. Coles also posted strong figures. Wesfarmers recorded sales of $13.6 billion, with Coles' same-store (comparing like with like) supermarket sales rising by 4.3 per cent, beating Woolworths' result for the twenty-fifth consecutive quarter. Bunnings' same-store sales rose by 8.2 per cent. Coles, like Woolworths, was continuing to increase its number of outlets, announcing a $1.1 billion investment in seventy new stores Australia-wide for the year.

Both chains recorded ongoing weaknesses in general merchandise and petrol sales, as ACCC rulings against them began to bite. Concerning the rise of Aldi, the supermarkets were publicly sanguine, contending that they had already suppressed their prices and were not in danger of suffering the same fate as Tesco and others in the United Kingdom. Richard Goyder, the managing director of Wesfarmers, said, 'We're driving very hard on our own-brand product range to make sure we're very competitive with Aldi – it's nothing like the price differential you see in the UK between the majors and Aldi.'

As these results were being announced, however, the adverse publicity for both companies showed no sign of abatement. Almost every week in the second half of 2014 seemed to bring a new story of alleged misbehaviour by Coles or Woolworths. On 19 August the ACCC mounted Federal Court action against the supermarkets' fuel outlets for their use of a petrol price-monitoring program called Informed Sources. Real-time monitoring, alleged the ACCC, might have been intended to provide transparency for customers' benefit but its actual effect was to enable the fuel retailers to tacitly collude in setting their prices, and to suppress competition by engaging in price wars against those who did not follow suit. The hearing was set for 2015; the ACCC's task was to show that by subscribing to the same price-monitoring service, the retailers were implicitly lessening competition.

The bad news cascaded through the last months of 2014. The Fair Work Ombudsman, Natalie James, said she was concerned the supermarket chains were not paying trolley workers fairly. 'Big companies sub-contracting out services on their sites have a responsibility to ensure those contracts do not undercut minimum employee entitlements,' Ms James said. 'This responsibility extends to supply-chain contractors. Just because a company doesn't "own" the contract doesn't mean it can wash its hands of it.' (Although, as we have seen in the Melissa Roch case against Coles' subcontracted security guards, washing its hands of contractors' problems is precisely what the supermarkets have been able to do.) The Fair Work Ombudsman was pursuing four cases before the courts, and in eleven previous cases since 2008 it had won more than $400,000 worth of underpaid wages for workers who had been paid as little as $5 an hour; one was a non-English speaker who had not been paid for six weeks. Ms James quoted census data showing that almost a third of Australia's 1500 trolley workers were younger than twenty, and almost half (40 per cent) did not have schooling beyond Year 10. A third were born outside Australia. 'They are at greater risk in that an unscrupulous employer may deliberately take advantage of their vulnerability,' Ms James said.

The themes of middle-management shortcomings that have been investigated in this book continued to surface. On 16 September 2014 the ACCC launched an action against Woolworths in the Federal Court, alleging that the company had systematically failed to withdraw from selling unsafe own-brand products, including the Abode 3L Stainless Steel Deep Fryer, Woolworths Select Drain Cleaner 1L and a ten-pack bundle of Safety Matches. (A woman had been burnt by oil after the deep fryer's handle snapped; a child had burned himself badly with the drain cleaner, which he opened due to an unsafe cap; and there were reports warning that igniting one match could set aflame the entire box.) In all cases, Woolworths had not withdrawn or recalled the products, inaction which the ACCC argued amounted to misleading advertising. It sought pecuniary penalties, declarations, injunctions, findings of fact, publicity orders, and orders that Woolworths implement a product safety compliance program and that Woolworths publish information to raise consumer awareness about product safety and how to report safety incidents.

On 29 September, after a long-running action launched by the ACCC, the Federal Court ordered Coles to cease for three years from advertising its bread as 'freshly baked' and 'baked today' when the dough had in fact been frozen. Bread under two brands – Cuisine Royale and Coles Bakery – had been advertised as freshly baked when in fact it had been made in Denmark, Germany and Ireland months earlier, frozen and shipped to Australia. Coles was also ordered to put up signage alerting customers to how it had misled them. It faced the prospect of up to $3 million in fines. A spokesman for Coles said, 'It was never Coles' intention to mislead our customers, but we accept that we could have done a better job in explaining how these products are made and we have already made changes to ensure customers are properly informed.' Jeff Kennett, speaking not as Coles' arbiter of supplier relationships but as the citizen who had previously championed the complaint against the misrepresentation of the bread, commented, 'I hope this stands as a shot across the bow of not only companies that sell and offer goods and services, but those companies that are contractors to deliver the advertising and promotion of their activities. The public are entitled to receive accurate information of things that they are being tempted or in the pursuit of purchasing.'

The wave of anti-supermarket feeling snowballed, a sign of a thoroughly lost public relations war. Woolworths was defending itself against accusations as diverse as ridiculing a transgender customer, stocking singlets with jingoistic messages, and discriminating against a blind woman through its website. The supermarkets would be forgiven for thinking they could not take a trick; winning on the balance sheet seemed to go together with losing on the public relations front.

Coles and Woolworths are as unpopular as they are successful. But should morality come into it? The distinction between intent and effect is perhaps the fundamental one. Noam Chomsky wrote, 'If you ask the CEO of some major corporation what he does, he will say, in all honesty, that he is slaving 20 hours a day to provide his customers with the best goods or services he can and creating the best possible conditions for his employees.' There is no evidence that this is not so even for the likes of John Durkan, who admitted to such widespread wrongdoing as leader of Coles' ARC program. No doubt Durkan and his team went, and still go, to work each day to do their best, as they saw it, for their customers, employees and shareholders.

Senator Nick Xenophon does not think the supermarkets are evil, in the sense of being run by people who mean ill. As a passionate opponent of poker machines, Xenophon took two women whose lives had been destroyed by gambling to meet Woolworths' CEO Grant O'Brien and the company's then chairman, the late James Strong. 'They were very decent,' says Xenophon, who also praises Coles and Woolworths for responding to his appeal to help employees of the broke Spring Valley company. 'They're not bad people. However, their ultimate attitude is that they have a responsibility to their shareholders. What you see is a function of their market power.'

While the structure of the corporation is designed to allay personal morality – Ambrose Bierce called it 'an ingenious device for obtaining profit without individual responsibility' – reform advocates such as Xenophon acknowledge that to witch-hunt individuals is to miss the point that concerns most Australians. It doesn't matter who is making the decisions; it is their effect on our communities that must be addressed. As Chomsky goes on: 'But then you take a look at what the corporation does, the effect of its legal structure, the vast inequalities in pay and conditions, and you see the reality is something far different.'

In Canberra, Xenophon's is a lonely voice. The public's disquiet about the supermarkets has not, in any significant way, pervaded the national capital. Occasionally Nationals pipe up on behalf of growers. Small business minister Bruce Billson has worked for the grocery code of conduct, to chip away at the excesses of supermarket power. Only the cross-benchers speak openly about giving courts the power to break up Coles and Woolworths. Major-party MPs have little to say. Two of Kevin Rudd's once-upon-a-time advisers, Alister Jordan and Andrew

Charlton, became executives at Wesfarmers. With former West Australian premier Alan Carpenter also on its payroll, Wesfarmers/Coles has been described as the pasture to which Rudd-era Labor types went out.

The Australian National Retailers' Association has lobbied Canberra successfully on the supermarkets' behalf. It has influenced public policy on specific issues such as trading hours, plastic bags, unit pricing and Grocery Watch, as well as more broadly on tax reform, the minimum wage, the carbon tax and consumer law. As a donor to political parties, Wesfarmers is invisible; Woolworths has given $186,000 over the past two years, split approximately 65:35 between the Coalition and Labor. Yet while they are not big donors, the supermarkets' role in the political money cycle is not to be ignored. According to the Australian Electoral Commission, affiliates of both major parties receive significant income from Coles and Woolworths through dividends, union dues and other payments. The Coalition, through its Melbourne-based Cormack Foundation, received $1.1 million from Wesfarmers and Woolworths in the past two years. On its members' behalf, the retail employees' union, the SDA, takes in more than $8 million a year from Wesfarmers and Woolworths. The supermarkets do not so much *give money to* the political parties as they *make money for* them, a role that embeds them all the deeper in the political establishment.

'They don't have to be big donors,' Xenophon says.

'They are all-pervasive, and that gives them the influence they need.'

Giving courts the power to force divestiture, as Xenophon advocates, does have support outside Canberra, and sometimes from unlikely quarters. The former Woolworths liquor chief and architect of the rise of Dan Murphy's, Tony Leon, agreed in late 2014 that the ACCC should have the power to break up the liquor giants, telling the *Australian Financial Review* that the supermarkets had too much influence in the market and 'it would be good for the industry' if the ACCC were able to forcibly break them up. But the ACCC chairman Rod Sims demurred, saying, 'I think it's too big a step to take, in my personal view. Obviously it's a policy issue for governments to think about that, but as a person who would be part of an organisation that would have to make that decision, I think it's too big a decision for a regulator to make.'

The market itself may turn out to be the reformers' friend. The supermarkets' popularity with politicians has rested in large part on their suppression of grocery prices. Xenophon says the supermarkets have 'overstated' their role in price deflation; certainly the global deflation of food prices after the GFC was helpful. But in 2014 there were signs of a turnaround. Woolworths boasted price deflation of around 2.9 per cent in 2012/13, and Coles 1.7 per cent, but in 2014 a Citigroup study found Woolworths had raised prices by between 1.3 and 8.7 per cent in May and June. Deutsche Bank's supermarket price index calculated rises of 3.3 per cent, 4.8 per cent and 5.4 per cent in the last three quarters of 2013/14. These rises had not been pushed by passing on suppliers' costs, but had gone to gross margins – in other words, they were decisions made by the supermarkets. The era of Woolworths and Coles as crusading price-cutters faces increasing challenges.

The impact of Aldi's rise on Coles and Woolworths is still to be seen, but either way it offers no cheer for food growers and manufacturers in Australia. The supermarket chains' legacy for food production is permanent, says Xenophon. 'The end result is that they are pushing Australian farmers off the land. Farmers who have contracts with them become like medieval serfs. They stop investing in their businesses. More and more imported produce comes in, and eventually prices go up.'

He states this as a fact rather than a moral condemnation. Thomas Jefferson said that 'Money, not morality, is the principle commerce of civilised nations', and perhaps nothing is as definitive a judgment upon Coles and Woolworths than the facts of how they make their money. According to a survey of Australian grocery sales in 2013/14 by the research company IRI-Aztec, the supermarkets sell $28 billion worth of fresh food, but their fastest-growing sectors are junk food and tobacco, which together make up $17 billion of sales. They sell $8.4 billion worth of cigarettes and tobacco, $2.5 billion in confectionery, and $2.1 billion in soft drinks. Their fastest-growing items are loose tobacco, chips, ice-cream, medicinal goods and cigarettes. They make three times as much revenue from ice-cream as from all health foods combined. Private brand sales now accounted for 30 per cent of bread and cakes, 25 per cent of chilled goods, including dairy, 19.5 per cent of general merchandise, and 15.7 per cent of frozen foods.

Heather Yeatman, president of the Public Health Association of Australia and a professor at the University of Wollongong's School of Health Services, told Fairfax Media, which obtained the report, that the data was 'very depressing'. 'If you look at the list of top products, it's basically a list of stimulants, nicotine and caffeine . . . It is in keeping with all the data and research we are seeing, which shows Australians have rising obesity and declining health driven by poor diet and eating habits.' Strip away all the trimmings, and this is what our greatest retail success stories are: our greatest purveyors of junk food, tobacco and alcohol, a mirror to the nation they serve.

It is difficult to speak of 'responses' or 'solutions' when the Australian public has done so much, over such a long period of time, to give Coles and Woolworths the dominance they enjoy. The way the two chains have absorbed and dismantled their competition for ten decades is accepted as part of the cut-and-thrust of business. Corner stores and little hardware shops fail because we let them fail. The supermarkets' seizure of retail space, overriding opposition from local communities and councils, has been proof of their superior funding, organisation and use of land and environment laws. Their control of malls at the expense of small businesses is a demonstration of the power that comes with size. When they have victimised employees or customers with whom they are in dispute, they have not always won the battle, but over time they win the war, driving deregulation of shopping hours and downward pressure on award wages that demands more, for less, from their workers. But they still employ 400,000 people. This alone gives them inexorable influence. Politicians in Canberra and unions representing staff are inside the supermarkets' tent; like the banks, Coles and Woolworths are perceived as too big to let fail.

For those who want Coles and Woolworths to change their ways, the question remains: *How?* Point to the popular action in Byron Bay to stop Dan Murphy's, but this came after 110 liquor licenses had already been issued in that shire. It was very much a rearguard action. Point to the ACCC case against Coles for unconscionable conduct, but this ultimately cost the supermarket, at most, 0.96 per cent of one year's profit. For several years' worth of bad corporate behaviour, Coles did not pay dearly. Giving courts the power to break up the supermarkets lacks sufficient backing in Canberra. All the reputational damage from the unconscionable conduct case and other bad-news stories has done nothing to turn political sentiment against the supermarkets.

And even if it were possible, would a forced break-up be effective? If Coles had to divest its hardware business, would this stop its supermarkets from screwing suppliers? If Woolworths spun off its liquor stores, would this make any difference to how it treated its milk or lamb farmers? A break-up might be disruptive to the supermarkets' strategic plans, and therefore unwanted by them, but as a means to achieving fairer outcomes for Australian food manufacturers and renewing investment in food production, its effect might be limited.

One desirable legislative action would be to make the grocery code of conduct mandatory. Businesses hate regulation, but in this case Coles and Woolworths have deserved it. They have shown over many years that they cannot be trusted to self-regulate their relationships with their suppliers. The AFGC's code is comprehensive and sensible, and it has been drafted by those who know what has been going on. It needs to be given teeth. If Coles and Woolworths are doing nothing wrong, they have nothing to fear.

Consumer boycotts, or other forms of concerted grassroots action, are often portrayed as responses in the only language corporations speak. There is the question of how many supermarket shoppers such a protest could round up in order to be effective, but let's assume it was possible. What effect would a consumer boycott have upon Colesworths?

Given that a decision to take your custom elsewhere does not come with a notice of motivation, the supermarkets would not necessarily understand that you had stopped shopping with them because you disagree with how they have treated dairy farmers. What the supermarkets would understand was that their sales and profits had declined. Their response to this has never been to wake up one day with a bad conscience. Instead, their response is to combat falling sales. In the United Kingdom and the United States, this has led them to compete with the German supermarkets and dollar stores in a race to the bottom. This means even worse news for producers. When Dick Smith says the future will be all Aldi and Walmart, he might add 'under the Coles and Woolworths names'. The Australian retailers have never been original thinkers. If necessary, they will imitate Aldi. They will copy success all the way, and a consumer boycott may unintentionally hasten the race to the nasty side of cheapness.

What is wrong with cheap, anyway? In the discussion of consumer action against supermarkets, one name is notably absent. Choice, the representative of the Australian Consumers' Association, has been relatively silent on Coles and Woolworths. That is because Choice is a watchdog for rip-offs and misleading conduct, and it has said in the past that it cannot really complain about the supermarkets when they have done so much to bring prices down. Therein lies the heart of the problem, if it is such. Consumer benefit is seen to be married to price. If you are paying less, you are better off. Woolworths and Coles have, through price deflation, made you better off from this traditional consumer point of view.

To challenge this, you have to take another point of view – such as by asking Nick Nikitaras' question, 'How expensive is that cheap product?' In other words, you'd have to form the view that, in an economy, different parts are related to each other in hidden ways that need to be investigated. This may lead to the conclusion that cheap products may cost thousands of jobs; they may ruin industries and communities; they may, somewhere down the line, cost you your own livelihood. A cheaper shopping basket today may have unforeseen consequences for you and your country tomorrow. This book has been an attempt to encourage that broader, interconnected perspective. When you buy that one-dollar milk, how much are you really paying?

Coles and Woolworths may be neither good nor evil, but they are undeniably enormous. An 'effects test' for anticompetitive behaviour, recommended by the Harper Review, represents a shift in thinking to one that recognises the amoral destructiveness of size: that some businesses are so big that they cannot help injuring a competitive marketplace, whether they want to or not. This size alone is enough to warrant changing the law to enforce an 'effects test'.

In April 2015, Master Grocers' Australia and Liquor Retailers Australia, representing the independent sector, laid the challenge at Canberra's feet: 'The battle to change Australia's competition laws will be hard fought. Two of Australia's biggest and wealthiest conglomerates don't want it. We believe this is an area where the federal government can show genuine leadership – to give the little guy the ability to grow their business and create jobs . . . [C]hange is urgent, the time to act is now.' Australians love the little guy but have rewarded the big.

What this drive towards enormity says about Australia is one of those straining tensions between myth and reality that have run through our history. We might like to see ourselves as local, but we behave big and corporate. In August 2014 Andrew Robb, the trade minister, said, 'We are an oligopoly community. We shouldn't fight it.' In Australia's history, even as painters were portraying gold-panners in creeks with their tents, wives and babies in the background, our mining industry had been taken over by capital-hungry corporations. We like to romanticise our relationship with our produce, but our actions betray us as a nation that rewards size and doesn't choose so much as follow, as a herd.

If we can't go into a mall without being hauled in by the duopoly – apples from Woolies, cereal from Coles, beer from Liquorland, wine from Dan Murphy's, a hammer from Bunnings, shoes from Kmart, ink from Office-works, a toy from Target, a pillow from Big W, petrol from Coles Express – then that shows the power we have given these two companies. As the AFGC's Gary Dawson says, 'Concentration is what it is, and it's not going to change in a hurry. We have got to make that work in as reasonable a fashion as we can.'

ACKNOWLEDGMENTS

Thanks:

Nick Feik, Chris Feik, Julian Welch, Imogen Kandel, Morry Schwartz and the staff at Black Inc.; Marco Nikitaras, Nick Nikitaras, Richard Flanagan, Libby Davidson, Russell Mahoney, Anna Kelly, Sandy Grant, Tricia Shantz, Guy Mallam, Dominic White, Stephen King, Stuart Knox, Geordie Williamson, Leela Sutton, the late James Strong, Mike Blacklock, Mike Logan, Gary Dawson, James Mathews, Brad Wehr, Sarah Collingwood, Tony Lutfi, and those other very helpful people who took the risk of speaking to me on condition of anonymity due to their continuing employment by or connections with the supermarket companies.

SOURCES

Sources are interviews with the author unless otherwise attributed. Following are the legal cases mentioned in the book.

CHAPTER 3

Woolworths Ltd v Blacktown City Council [2011] NSWLEC 1296

Woolworths Ltd and City of Joondalup [2009] WASAT 41

Woolworths Ltd v The Commissioner of Police [2013] WASC 413

Woolworths Ltd v Director of Liquor Licensing [2013]
     WASCA 227

Woolworths Limited [2013] SALC 23

Woolworths Limited v Smithfield Hotel Pty Ltd [2012] SALC 57

Australian Competition and Consumer Commission v Liquorland
     (Australia) Pty Ltd [2006] FCA 826

Australian Competition and Consumer Commission v Liquorland
     (Australia) Pty Ltd (ACN 007 512 419) [2005] FCA 683

Australian Competition and Consumer Commission v Liquorland
     (Australia) Pty Limited [2006] FCA 1799

Australian Competition and Consumer Commission v Liquorland
     (Australia) Pty Ltd [2005] FCA 524

Chapter 4

Woolworths Limited v Shop Distributive & Allied Employees
    Association (Queensland Branch) Union of Employees
    [2010] FCAFC 29

Woolworths Ltd v Sisko [2013] NSWWCCPD 38

Woolworths Limited v Buckland [2012] NSWWCCPD 57

Warfe v Woolworths (Vic) Pty Ltd [2011] VCC 1517

Woolworths Ltd v Warfe [2013] VSCA 22

P Pushie v Woolworths Ltd [2013] VCC 863

Woolworths Limited v Christopher-Coates [2014]
    NSWWCCPD 14

Homes v Coles Group Limited [2014] FWC 1013

Nicolaides v Coles Supermarkets Australia Pty Ltd & Ors [2013]
    VCC 1343

Coles Supermarkets Pty Ltd v Bourchdan [2009]
    NSWWCCPD 116

Robinson v Woolworths Limited [2012] FWA 1179

Lawrie v Coles Supermarkets Australia Pty Ltd [2008] SAIRC 54

Haleluka v Coles Supermarkets Australia Pty Ltd [2011]
    NSWDC 47

Coles Supermarkets Australia Pty Limited v Haleluka [2012]
    NSWCA 343

Coles Supermarkets Australia Pty Ltd v Clarke [2013]
    NSWCA 272

Strong v Woolworths Ltd [2012] HCA 5

Strong v Woolworths Limited T/as Big W & Anor [2011]
    HCATrans 131

Strong v Woolworths Limited T/as Big W & Anor [2011]

HCATrans 194

Woolworths Limited v Strong & Anor [2010] NSWCA 282

Woolworths Limited v Strong (No 2) [2011] NSWCA 72

Roch v Coles Supermarkets Australia Pty Ltd & Anor [2011]
VCC 1487

Roch v Coles Supermarkets Australia Pty Ltd [2012] VCC 185

Tormey v Coles Supermarket [2008] NSWDC 67

Coles Supermarkets Australia Pty Ltd v Tormey [2009]
NSWCA 135

Svajcer v Woolworths Limited [2014] VCC 159

CHAPTER 5

Woolworths Limited v Mark Konrad Olson and Anor [2004]
NSWSC 849

Woolworths Limited v Mark Konrad Olson [2004] NSWCA 372

Australian Competition and Consumer Commission v Coles
Supermarkets Australia Pty Ltd [2014] FCA 1405

'Required reading for
every Australian who
seriously cares about
the fair go enduring.'
—Peter FitzSimons

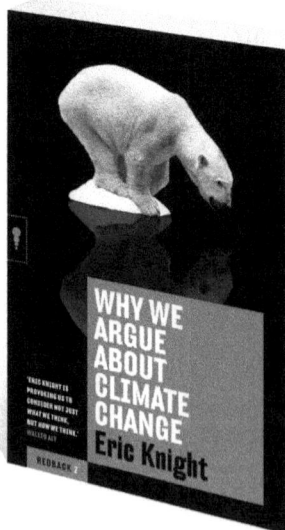

'Eric Knight is provoking
us to consider not just
what we think, but
how we think.'
—Waleed Aly

SHORT BOOKS ON BIG ISSUES BY
LEADING AUSTRALIAN WRITERS AND THINKERS

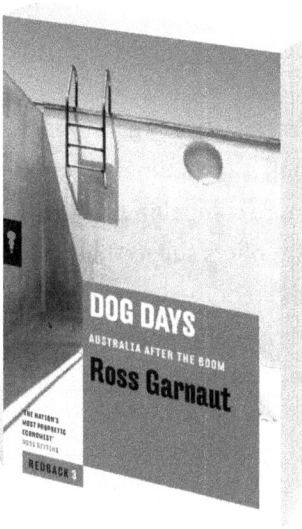

'This book is a must-read for anyone concerned with the economic and social future of Australia . . . lucid, compelling and unburdened by political bias.'
—Bob Hawke

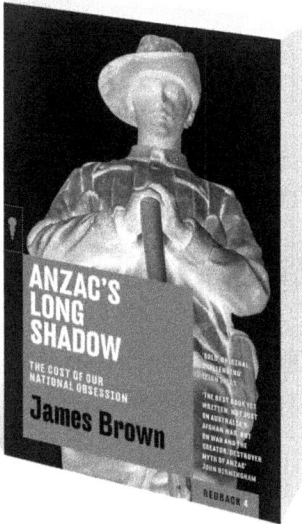

'The best book yet written, not just on Australia's Afghan war, but on war itself and the creator/destroyer myth of Anzac.'
—John Birmingham

CRIME & PUNISHMENT
OFFENDERS AND VICTIMS
IN A BROKEN JUSTICE SYSTEM

Russell Marks

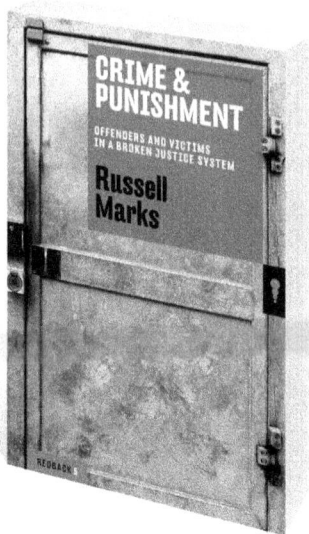

'A reflective, well-argued book . . . what makes it even more compelling is Marks also offers suggestions on a different (better) system of crime and punishment.'
—*Sydney Morning Herald*

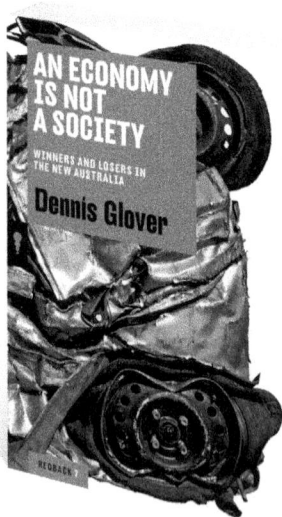

AN ECONOMY IS NOT A SOCIETY
WINNERS AND LOSERS IN
THE NEW AUSTRALIA

Dennis Glover

In modern Australia, productivity is all that matters, our leaders tell us. Economic growth above all else. But is this really what we, the people, want? Does it make our lives and our communities better?